Black Women in Science

Black Women IN SCIENCE

A BLACK HISTORY BOOK FOR KIDS

Kimberly Brown Pellum, PhD

Foreword by Dr. Rosetta A. Conner

Illustrations by Keisha Morris

ROCKRIDGE PRESS

Interior and Cover Designer: Will Mack
Art Producer: Sue Bischofberger
Editor: Mary Colgan
Production Manager: Oriana Siska
Production Editors: Melissa Edeburn and Erum Khan

Illustrations © 2019 Keisha Morris
Author Photo credit: @jaybimagelab on Instagram

ISBN: Print 978-1-64152-707-1 | eBook 978-1-64152-708-8

R1

Printed in China

This book is dedicated to my mother, Linda Grace Brown. When I gave birth to my own baby, I was cared for by the nurses my mom taught during her 40-year career. What a feeling to know that the warm and expert care I received was, in large part, due to the woman who has always warmed, covered, and loved my siblings and me. Her work as a nurse and instructor of nursing has been a superb example of service-oriented science. With degrees from Temple University and Tuskegee University, which has a long record of excellence in STEM, Mama has always used her extensive knowledge in medicine to help others. Her approach to her career is a great lesson for many about choosing a purpose-filled profession. When I bump into young nurses who exclaim, "Your mom taught me!" it tells me that some immaterial thing she gave them helped them gain employment and thinking of her still gets them excited. I could not be more proud. Mama, thank you for being our family physician, agriculturalist, and my first black woman in science pioneer!

Contents

Foreword

I am smart. I am a veterinarian. I am a woman. I am black. Like many of the amazing black women you will learn about throughout your reading, I have worked hard to achieve goals in my life and career. The path was not always easy, but no achievement worth having ever will be.

I've not always known I wanted to be a veterinarian. I have, on the other hand, always known I loved science and math. When I was a young girl growing up in Waycross, Georgia, I excelled in all of my math and science classes. The challenges of solving a math equation or understanding the ecosystem were so fulfilling. This tiny spark of passion for math and science was ignited early on and helped fuel my decision to pursue a career that would combine the two. I set out on a path that led me to Florida Agricultural and Mechanical University (FAMU) in fall 2000.

I began my journey as a pharmacy student, studying and working tirelessly to obtain my degree. College was a time of exploration. It allowed me to learn about life and decision making. So much growth happened during this time. I was faced with a big decision that would change my life. Although I was a good student who worked hard, I found out that being a pharmacy major just wasn't for me. I either had to change my course of study or continue on an unfulfilling path. I decided to major in animal science, but I still had no idea I would, one day, become a veterinarian. I graduated from FAMU in 2005 with a Bachelor of Science degree in animal science. Then, I worked for a veterinarian as a veterinary assistant. It was through this experience that I knew I had found my place. I loved it! The following year, I applied and was accepted into the veterinary school at Tuskegee University.

The first and only veterinary program in the nation at a Historically Black University is found in Tuskegee, Alabama. Tuskegee Institute School of Veterinary Medicine was established in 1945 by Dr. Frederick Douglass Patterson. More than 70 percent of African-American veterinarians in the United States today graduated from Tuskegee University College of Veterinary Medicine (TUCVM). I am one of those fortunate veterinarians able to call TUCVM my alma mater. So many amazing black women who matriculated at Tuskegee paved the way for me, including Dr. Alfreda Johnson Webb, the first female graduate of Tuskegee Institute School of Veterinary Medicine; Dr. Ruby Perry, the first black female board-certified veterinary radiologist and current dean of TUCVM; and Dr. Erika Gibson, the first black board-certified veterinary neurosurgeon.

Upon completion of my Doctor of Veterinary Medicine degree in 2010, I moved to Atlanta, Georgia, to begin my career as a veterinarian. I have spent my career as a general practitioner, focusing on small companion animals (dogs and cats). I am able to educate people about the importance of preventive medicine for their pets. I provide medical intervention when pets are sick. Performing a variety of surgical procedures on pets is one of my favorite aspects of my career. I also love the challenge of determining what may be causing certain behaviors in pets. My personal interactions with people allow for the betterment of so many animals' lives. What I really like most about the field of veterinary medicine is that, with my degree, I can work with *any* animal species that is not human!

The field of veterinary medicine offers so many possibilities—from teaching future veterinarians, to general practice, to specializing in a certain aspect of medicine for animals; and from working in a research laboratory, aquarium, or zoo, to working on a ranch or a nature preserve in a foreign country. The possibilities are almost endless. Veterinary medicine is one of many science, technology, engineering, and math (STEM) careers that need gender and ethnicity diversity for its continued growth and sustainability.

As you read this book, I hope you understand your worth. You are the future of STEM. You will bring the fresh ideas, unique perspectives, gentle nature, and bold fierceness needed to tackle our world's big equations. There is an invention waiting to be innovated and a first waiting to be accomplished with your name on it! Even if you do not know exactly what you want to be when you grow up, just remember to explore and have fun learning. Let your passion guide your path. I cannot wait to see what you will do. You are smart. You are important. You can become anything.

Yours in the pursuit of learning,

Dr. Rosetta A. Conner

Bachelor of Science in Animal Science,
Florida Agricultural and Mechanical University
Doctor of Veterinary Medicine,
Tuskegee University School of Veterinary Medicine

Introduction

Imagine a world of endless possibilities—a world where wonder and curiosity guide you. Your thoughts and questions are uninhibited, and every step in your investigation evokes excitement. Welcome to the world of science.

It is my hope that this book warmly invites you to join this world. Do not be intimidated. Each biography has been crafted to educate and inspire you. Furthermore, every woman's profile offers a road map for successfully navigating the science arena. Remember Dr. Rebecca Crumpler when the odds are against you. Carry yourself with the confidence of Bessie Coleman. Use your gifts to destroy inequality like Mamie Clark. Approach every task with excellence in mind like Katherine Johnson. And, when you are fearful, think of Mae Jemison.

Although you may think you have nothing in common with these trailblazers, you do. Just like you, they, too, were young and full of brilliance and potential. Everything you need to succeed is already inside of you. Their stories are here to nurture your existing talents. Your path to success may not be easy. On the contrary, as you advance in your field, you may sometimes feel uncomfortable. Others in the room may not look like you. Do not be discouraged. We have been waiting for a bright, insightful scholar just like you, and your gifts are needed to continue the legacies of the pioneers in these pages.

I hope you are ready to experience the adventures I describe here.

Let the journey begin.

Rebecca Lee CRUMPLER

{ 1831–1895 }

The Civil War was a violent four-year feud between Northern and Southern states about whether slavery should continue in the United States. At the end of the war—in 1865—about four million Africans in the United States were freed. However, a year before slavery's end, Rebecca Lee Crumpler had already become the first African-American woman to work as a professional medical doctor. Later, she also provided care for those formerly enslaved through an arrangement with the government. She became the only woman doctor to write a book in the nineteenth century.

Rebecca was born Rebecca Davis in Delaware in 1831, and she was raised in Pennsylvania by her aunt, who was known to care for sick neighbors. Both states had ended slavery much earlier than the rest of the United States, allowing their residents of African descent to lead more enriching lives and explore their talents and skills on their own terms. Although she was not formally trained, Rebecca's aunt used her knowledge of remedies and healing techniques to serve the African-American community in Pennsylvania. Her work almost certainly inspired young Rebecca to care for others by practicing medicine.

Described as a "special student in mathematics," Rebecca was a sharp thinker who chased opportunity. She worked as a nurse for various doctors for a number of years before moving to Charlestown, Massachusetts, at the age of 21. At that time, official nursing schools had not yet opened, so she acquired the knowledge she needed to care for the ill through the one-on-one experiences she had with her many patients.

New England Female Medical College, first called Boston Female Medical College, was the first medical college for women in the world. Male physicians often mocked the school and the idea of women as doctors. Many thought women lacked the intelligence needed to work in a field that required such a demanding education. Some also thought women were too weak to handle the challenges of medicine and medical emergencies. But Rebecca trusted her abilities. She had letters of recommendation from the doctors she worked for and applied to the college. She was admitted in 1860.

Most professional schools usually rejected both women and African-American applicants. So, schools that did allow African-American women were few and had mostly white students. This environment did not stop Rebecca from plunging into the four-year

"IT MAY BE WELL TO STATE HERE THAT, HAVING BEEN REARED BY A KIND AUNT IN PENNSYLVANIA, WHOSE USEFULNESS WITH THE SICK WAS CONTINUALLY SOUGHT, I EARLY CONCEIVED A LIKING FOR, AND SOUGHT EVERY OPPORTUNITY TO RELIEVE THE SUFFERINGS OF OTHERS."

curriculum at the New England Female Medical College. She took courses in theory, chemistry, therapeutics, anatomy, medical jurisprudence, obstetrics, diseases of women and children, physiology, and hygiene. Her coursework called for 17 weeks of study—for 30 or more hours per week—during the first year of instruction. Students were also required to apprentice for physicians. In addition to her hefty workload, Rebecca dealt with a heartbreaking loss. Her first husband, Wyatt Lee, a former slave, died of tuberculosis while she was in school.

Rebecca pressed on, and, by February 1864, she and two white classmates, Mary Lockwood Allen and Elizabeth Kimball, had finished the thesis papers required to move to the final stage of the program. Now they had to complete oral examinations in front of four faculty members. Although each young woman was ultimately recommended for graduation, the faculty committee claimed there were shortcomings in Rebecca's education and that she had made "slow progress" during her time there. They wrote, "Some of us have hesitated very seriously in recommending her." Despite such comments, the college's board of trustees decided she was worthy of graduating and granted her the degree. This made Rebecca the first African-American woman medical doctor. Still, even as she graduated, the school attached her race to her name; they referred to her as "Mrs. Rebecca Lee, negress."

After graduation, Rebecca stayed in Boston to practice medicine as well as seek further training. She wanted to be well informed and provide the best possible care for her patients. Like her aunt had done, Rebecca committed herself to caring for those who needed the most help. She focused on women's and children's issues, especially among the less fortunate. In 1865, when the Civil War ended, she moved to Richmond, Virginia, to do what she saw as "real missionary work." She worked with the Freedmen's Bureau, an agency created by Congress to help millions of formerly enslaved Africans and poor whites in the South recover from enslavement and the devastation caused by the war.

Providing this type of assistance was deeply personal to Rebecca. Her second husband, Arthur Crumpler, was a former fugitive slave from Southampton County, Virginia. The Freedmen's Bureau provided food and housing, established schools, and offered legal and medical aid to people like Arthur. This was important because most African Americans had no access to health care while enslaved. After emancipation, Rebecca and other African-American physicians sprang into action to serve the people who had been enslaved.

The rising need for more doctors to care for newly freed black people inspired others to gain medical training. The first African-American medical schools in the United States, such as Howard University Medical School in Washington, DC, were established to train black people for careers as doctors. Although African-American doctors were essential after the war, they were usually shunned.

Rebecca faced much discrimination in Richmond, Virginia—the old capital of the Confederacy. Various sources say that "men doctors snubbed [Rebecca], druggists balked at filling her prescriptions, and some people wisecracked that the M.D. behind her name stood for nothing more than 'Mule Driver.'" Rebecca was not deterred by such challenges. Her calling to serve was bigger than the racist and sexist bullies she encountered. Caring for the sick was the most important thing in her life. She treated countless people, regardless of their class, among Richmond's population of more than 30,000 people of color.

By 1869, Rebecca had returned to Boston, where she had trained to become a doctor. She lived and practiced medicine on Beacon Hill—a mainly African-American neighborhood—before moving to Hyde Park, Massachusetts, in 1880. While no longer actively practicing medicine, Rebecca continued making contributions to society. Three years later, she published *A Book of Medical Discourse,* one of the first publications written by an African American about medicine. It was also the only text written by a woman physician in the nineteenth century. The book showed Rebecca's dedication to society's most vulnerable people, providing advice on the medical care of women and children.

The trailblazing doctor died in 1895, but her legacy endured. The Rebecca Lee Society, one of the first medical societies for African-American women, was named after her, and her old home in Boston is a stop on the Women's Heritage Trail. The Rebecca Lee Pre-Health Society at Syracuse University is so named as a nod to her remarkable life. The goal of the group is to help students succeed in medicine by providing resources and mentors.

Rebecca's support of homeopathy had a positive impact on how other physicians helped prevent disease. *Homeo* means "same." Homeopathic medicine calls for exposing healthy patients to certain illnesses in very small doses to boost their immunity from the same sickness. This approach is used today when treating many sicknesses, such as the flu.

EXPLORE MORE! Search online or at your local library to learn about the first African-American nurse, Mary Eliza Mahoney, and other early pioneers in medicine.

TIPS FOR YOU! Rebecca Crumpler's aunt inspired her to pursue a career in medicine. Who in your family inspires you? Write them a thank-you note, and explain why you appreciate what they do.

Annie Turnbo MALONE

{1869–1957}

Annie Turnbo Malone was a chemist and businesswoman whose brilliant achievements in the beauty industry helped her become the first African-American female millionaire. She developed a successful line of personal hygiene and beauty products designed especially for black women. She also held the first US patent for a hot comb. Annie's most popular product was a potion she called the Wonderful Hair Grower. Her desire to educate others and expand her business inspired her to build the famous Poro College of St. Louis. The cosmetology school and its franchises employed about 75,000 women in North and South America, Africa, and the Philippines. Annie's business was the first global African-American beauty and hair-care brand.

Annie's mother and father had been enslaved. Her father, Robert Turnbo, fought for the Union during the Civil War. Her mother, Isabella, escaped with their children from Kentucky, where slavery was still permitted.

By way of the Ohio River, they found safety in Metropolis, Illinois, where Annie was born. Annie was the 10th of 11 children; she was raised by an older sister after their parents died.

Annie showed promise in her science classes, but she had to leave high school because she was often sick. She had always been fascinated by hair. Inspired by an aunt who specialized in working with herbs, young Annie began experimenting with different ingredients to create new hair-care products for black women.

Annie grew up during a time when African-American women were starting to straighten their hair rather than wear it in natural styles, such as braided cornrows; this was because American society associated those styles with plantation work. Most blacks simply wanted to be treated as equals to white people. Others felt pressure to look more like white people to get jobs. In some cases, black people with straighter or wavy hair were treated better than those with curlier hair. For this reason, straightened hair became a symbol of success and sophistication for many black communities. This trend certainly influenced Annie's early products.

Hair care was also personal for the budding entrepreneur. Annie saw women using bacon grease, heavy oils, and butter to achieve their uncoiled looks. Others used combinations of lye and potatoes. She knew these methods damaged the hair and scalp. She also knew that harsh, alcohol-based potions destroyed the hair follicles and skin. She developed a line of less damaging hair-straightening and growth-stimulating hair products and began selling them door to door. Her motto for her Wonderful Hair Grower was "Clean scalps mean clean bodies!"

In 1902, Annie brought along her flair for business when she moved to St. Louis, Missouri. Not only did St. Louis host the World's Fair that year, it was also home to a thriving African-American population. Many had migrated from the South to find work and escape racial terror. The 25-year-old entrepreneur took advantage of the new opportunities and opened a store. Her customers liked her products so much that she decided to expand her business. Annie hired assistants and trained them to go door to door to distribute her products all over the country. She and her team also traveled to provide free hair treatments and tutorials at African-American churches, women's social clubs, and community centers. The tours helped women who may not have otherwise had access to professional hair services, but they were dangerous to Annie and her employees. White residents of many cities, especially in the South, tormented African-American visitors. Still, Annie felt her work was worth the risk. She organized press conferences and advertised in black newspapers.

Annie's work paid off. Her recruits recruited other recruits, and they recruited others, and so on. They appreciated the opportunity to earn money, and Annie rewarded good work with prizes like diamond rings.

"PORO COLLEGE IS MORE THAN A MERE BUSINESS ENTERPRISE. FOSTERING IDEALS OF PERSONAL BEAUTY AND TIDINESS, SELF-RESPECT, THRIFT AND INDUSTRY, AND TOUCHING THE LIVES OF MILLIONS."

Annie also made sure that her agents had access to the latest hair-care technology, such as pressing, curling, and waving irons, combs, and crimpers in various sizes. Her enterprise grew rapidly and even attracted famous guitarist Chuck Berry before he made it big in music.

One of her most celebrated trainees was Madam C. J. Walker, a former washerwoman who eventually established her own company that was similar to Annie's. While Walker is often thought of as the first African-American female millionaire, Annie actually reached the rank earlier. People often confused the brands because Walker launched a product called Wonderful Hair Straightener; an irritated Annie called Walker's concoction a fraudulent imitation. To discourage others from mimicking her products and sales tactics, in 1906, she trademarked her goods and services under the name Poro. Many people have suggested that she took the name from a West African group known for its emphasis on improving one's looks, body, and spirit. One of Annie's promotional booklets declares, "The name 'Poro' has come to stand as a mark of our service to the Race, a service that is economic, inspirational, [and] religious."

Annie's creative and intellectual ideas came together in her most important achievement: Poro College. In 1918, as her business boomed, she oversaw the opening of a state-of-the-art facility in St. Louis's elite African-American neighborhood. The facility contained the business's office, manufacturing headquarters, a cosmetology training center, and halls for civic, religious, and social events. Products were shipped directly from this facility. Annie's goal was for orders to be shipped the same day they were placed. She saw her property as a community space and made it available for African-American events that white-owned hotels and other venues refused to host. Several important organizations, including Booker T. Washington's National Negro Business League, used it for meetings and parties.

Annie was a champion of social responsibility. With 75,000 agents around the world and Poro schools in 32 cities, she had earned an estimated $14 million. She shared the money with employees, family, YMCAs, and other African-American colleges. She donated $25,000 to Tuskegee Institute and the same amount to Howard University's School of Medicine. She gave her agents cash for buying homes and maintained tennis courts for employee use.

Scarcity caused by the Great Depression, combined with Annie's generosity with her family, employees, and community, crippled her finances. Her husband attempted to take half her wealth in court during their divorce, but he was awarded only $20,000. Annie was forced to leave her cherished property and move her business to Chicago in 1930. A former employee took her to court, claiming that Annie had stolen her ideas. Several tax disputes with the US government made her situation even worse. As a result of so many misfortunes, Annie's reputation began to fall.

Annie's sinking career helped make room for Madam C. J. Walker's popularity. Buyers loved the rags-to-riches story Walker used to promote her brand. Her advertisements featured attractive and glitzy photographs of herself. They caught the attention of customers who wanted to be part of the glamorous style of the New Negro Renaissance. Walker's astonishing financial success encouraged white beauty companies to imitate her sales tactics. Walker began to overshadow her teacher. She improved upon the hot comb Annie had patented by widening the teeth to make it work better on black people's hair.

These setbacks did not stop Annie. She continued to work on her business until she died in 1957 at age 87. By that time, though, most of her money was gone. She had no children, so her estate, valued at $100,000, was left to her nieces and nephews.

Long before America began to embrace the idea of African Americans as full citizens—let alone as beauty consumers—Annie offered face powders in five different shades of brown. Not long after the end of slavery, Annie provided respectable and profitable work for black women who would otherwise have had few employment options. She showed that hair care and cosmetology could be paths to financial success and, thus, freedom.

Annie's legacy goes beyond her role as a businesswoman. Her commitment to her employees' welfare and to her community set an example for future business leaders. The St. Louis Colored Orphans Home was renamed the Annie Turnbo Malone Children and Family Service Center, and it continues to provide support for the city's youth. The street on which it is located is named in her honor.

EXPLORE MORE! Want to know Annie better? Visit https://www.freemaninstitute.com/poro.htm.

TIPS FOR YOU! Annie Malone rewarded her employees' good work. What's something you do well that makes people's lives better? (Cook? Do hair? Babysit?) Do it this week, then give yourself a treat or a tip based on how well you think you did.

Bessie COLEMAN

{ 1892–1926 }

Bessie Coleman's mastery of mechanics, technology, and aviation fueled her quest to empower African Americans in the air and on the ground. Bessie was the first black woman with a pilot's license, and she used her talent and popularity as an aviatrix stunt performer to create change. Although she only lived to be 34 years of age, her crowd-stirring flights, international merit awards, and deep desire to teach others firmly set her legacy as a pioneer who flew above barriers.

Bessie was born on January 26, 1892, in Atlanta, Texas—one of 13 children. Like many poor Southern black families at the time, hers picked cotton to get by. Her mother made sure the children took advantage of a traveling library that stopped in town a few times a year. Because of this, Bessie read often and developed a big imagination. She finished high school and even went on to college, which was rare for most Americans during the early 1900s. She worked hard as a laundress,

"YOU TELL THE WORLD I'M COMING BACK!"

saved her money, and enrolled in Oklahoma's Langston Industrial College, now known as Langston University.

Unfortunately, she had to leave college after just one semester when her money ran out. She decided to head for Chicago. Many African Americans were moving there to escape the racial violence and lack of employment that stained the South. That turned out to be a good decision. Chicago offered opportunity and a lively network. In 1915, she enrolled in the Burnham School of Beauty Culture, where she took a course in manicuring. Soon after, she became known as the best manicurist in black Chicago, impressing people with her speed and skill. Male customers waited to sit at the stunning young woman's table. She soon became a nail specialist at the White Sox Barber Shop, owned by the trainer of Chicago's American League Baseball Club.

But Chicago was not perfect. Although racism was mostly associated with the South, it existed all over the country. In the summer of 1919, a terrible riot broke out in the city after a group of whites stoned and drowned an African-American boy whose raft had drifted into an area of Lake Michigan designated for white use only. It took the National Guard four days to restore order to the city. During that time,

38 people died, hundreds were injured, and countless homes were destroyed. Bessie observed how racism hurt African Americans in other ways, too. She saw her brothers go off to serve the United States in World War I yet be treated as second-class citizens when they returned. This never sat well with her.

Seeing images of planes in news stories about the war, Bessie imagined that aviation might be a way to create a better life for herself and others like her. Her brothers shared stories about their time in France, noting that French women could learn to fly and that she could not. She decided to prove them wrong. She applied for flight schools across the United States. None accepted her because of her race and gender. Bessie was a big fan of the black newspaper the *Chicago Defender*, and had become friends with its founder, Robert Abbott. He suggested she try getting into an aviation school in France. She began taking French classes at night so she could complete her applications.

In November 1920, with the savings from her manicurist job and her job in a chili parlor, Coleman left Chicago and took a boat to France. There, she was accepted by the Caudron Brothers' School of Aviation. In flight school, she learned looping, tailspins, and landing. She also learned how dangerous flying could be when a classmate died in an accident. Coleman even had to sign a waiver stating she knew she could die if something went wrong. But Bessie didn't let the risks stop her.

On June 15, 1921, she received her international pilot's license from the *Federation Aéronautique Internationale* in France. She was the first American of any race or gender to do so. She had learned all about plane engines and parts and proven herself capable of a wide range of operational skills and life-saving air maneuvers. When she returned to the States on an ocean liner, reporters from several national African-American newspapers eagerly welcomed her. This was the beginning of her rise to fame.

Despite the warm welcome from newspaper reporters, many African Americans did not have a positive view of aviation. Just weeks before Bessie had earned her pilot's license, the Tulsa Race Riot took place in Tulsa, Oklahoma. The Greenwood District of Tulsa had been known as "Black Wall Street" because of its thriving banks, businesses, and successful African-American residents. However, on June 1, 1921, a mob of white people launched a full-scale assault on the district, which ended with white pilots dropping bombs on the community. The incident left dozens dead and countless more without homes. This was the first time airplanes had ever been used in an attack on US soil. The tragedy caused many black people to distrust planes and pilots.

Furthermore, American aviation was still not available to most blacks. Bessie wanted to change this. While in France, she had attended W. E. B. DuBois's Second Pan-African Congress in Paris. DuBois, an

African-American scholar and activist, used the meeting to promote unity for Africans around the world. Bessie decided then to use her flights to honor and promote African-American causes. She wanted to purchase her own plane and open a black flight school.

Despite her best efforts, commercial aviation companies refused to hire her, and plane suppliers refused to sell to her. She again turned to Europe for opportunities. She visited France, Germany, Holland, and Switzerland, studying with famous World War I master pilots and plane designers. She came back to the United States an even more remarkable aviatrix who could fly airplanes as well as war-tested veterans. When she arrived in New York in August 1922, the *New York Times* printed that she was "leading French and Dutch aviators as one of the best flyers they had seen." She told the press she planned to continue flying to inspire her people.

People began to call her "Queen Bess," and she was offered movie roles. She accepted one, believing it would boost her career. However, she backed out when she learned she would have to appear in torn clothing with a walking stick and a sack on her back. She refused to play out negative stereotypes of African Americans. Black celebrities cheered her on. In fact, the cast of *Shuffle Along*, a highly popular Broadway play that later starred Paul Robeson and Bessie's friend Josephine Baker, presented her with a silver trophy cup to acknowledge her hard work and determination.

Bessie gave the cup to her mother to thank her for the sacrifices she had made for her children.

Bessie arranged numerous air shows to raise money for her flight school. In an air show, pilots demonstrate aerial maneuvers and tricks to entertain an audience. Bessie's first air show took place on September 3, 1922, at Garden City in Long Island, New York. She dedicated her performance to the 15th Infantry Regiment, one of the first African-American brigades sent to France during World War I. A band played "The Star-Spangled Banner," and she was escorted to her plane, which she had borrowed from a rental company. She performed spirals and loops, and an officer in the Universal Negro Improvement Association parachuted from the wing of her plane. The crowd burst into excited applause. Bessie ended the show by taking passengers for a ride for $5 each.

Her second exhibition was at the annual Tri-State Fair in Memphis, Tennessee, where she was the main opening-day attraction. When her plane faltered and stopped midair, she amazed the crowd with a fast recovery.

Her third exhibition was in her beloved Chicago, where 2,000 people gathered at Checkerboard Field, a popular flight facility in one of America's biggest cities. She dedicated that performance to an African-American military group, the Eighth Infantry Regiment. Her favorite newspaper, the *Chicago Defender,* celebrated her as "The Only Race Aviatrix in the World."

Bessie's sister, Georgia, sat with her in the cockpit in a colorful costume that Bessie had bought for her. Bessie announced that her sister would parachute from 2,000 feet, but Georgia refused. A niece recalled them arguing, with Georgia fussing, "I don't care what you have bought. I'm not jumping out of no plane!" The audience cheered when Queen Bess landed perfectly, despite a near crash earlier in the show. Now known as "Brave Bessie," her career continued to soar.

Queen Bess appealed to almost everybody. She was attractive and petite and fun to watch. Her shows, with their aerial acrobatics, wing walking, parachuting, and diving, drew enormous crowds. They were also risky. By 1923, she had finally raised enough money to purchase her own plane—a surplus military "Jenny." She was going to use her prized plane to drop promotional materials for a tire company from the sky. Unfortunately, her plane's motor stopped moments after her ascent. It crashed into the ground, and Bessie suffered a broken leg, fragmented ribs, and several cuts to her face. She proved her tough spirit when she told a reporter, "Tell the world I'm coming back!" It took her three months in the hospital and several more for rest and recovery, but she returned to flying just as she'd promised.

While she recuperated, she lectured at the YMCA to bring in much-needed money. She also enjoyed Chicago's society life and mingled with stars such as singer/dancer Josephine Baker and actor William

"Bojangles" Robinson. Baker and Bessie became good friends, chatting easily in French. Inspired by Bessie, Baker, too, went to France to learn to fly.

Bessie's comeback performance was scheduled to take place at the state fairgrounds in Columbus, Ohio, on a day when the Ku Klux Klan was also holding a celebration at that venue. Bessie's performance was canceled because of all-day rain, but the KKK's event went ahead. Bessie rescheduled her performance and had a successful show. She then decided it was time to tour the South and raise funds for her longtime dream of opening an African-American flight school.

Bessie was not afraid of racism in the South. As far as she was concerned, it existed everywhere. On June 21, 1925, she held a showcase in her home state of Texas to commemorate Juneteenth, a holiday celebrating the emancipation of the enslaved. She refused to follow rules that called for separate entrances for African Americans and whites. Instead, she demanded one entrance for all. *The Houston Informer* reported that it was "the first time colored public of the South had been given the opportunity to fly."

At one show on her tour, a parachutist decided not to jump, so Bessie strapped on the gear and did it herself. She was in high demand and made appearances in cities all over the South. Between shows, she visited black churches and theaters to speak about her time overseas and her daredevil career. She also showed films of her adventures.

Bessie was still determined to open a flight school. While touring in Florida, she opened a beauty shop to help fund her dream. In a letter to her sister, she said the business had made almost enough money to build the school. Her exhibitions were starting to bring in more revenue, too. Her next show was scheduled for May 1, 1926, in Jacksonville, Florida. This was the same year that historian Carter D. Woodson founded Negro History Week, now called Black History Month.

Then things took a terrible turn. On April 30, 1926, Bessie and her mechanic, a white man named William Willis, took their plane for a test run. Willis was piloting while Bessie scoped out the ground and planned the show from the passenger's seat. A loose wrench became stuck in the engine and Willis lost control.

During this time, most planes had no roofs. Bessie and Willis fell to their deaths. People were heartbroken, and many communities across the country held memorials. Famous activist Ida B. Wells gave the eulogy at Bessie's funeral in Chicago. A group of uniformed pallbearers, who were veterans of the African Eighth Infantry Regiment, escorted her US flag–covered casket to its final resting place.

Bessie never saw her school open during her lifetime, but Lieutenant William J. Powell established the Bessie Coleman Aero Club in Los Angeles in 1929. By 1977, a group of black female pilots formed the Bessie Coleman Aviators Club, and, in 1995, the US Postal Service released the Bessie Coleman stamp. The Chicago

O'Hare Airport's address is 1000 Bessie Coleman Drive. Each year, on the anniversary of her death, African-American pilots fly over her grave and drop flowers in her honor.

EXPLORE MORE! Check out all the African-American heritage stamps offered at the United States Postal Service. Head to an office near you, or find them at www.usps.gov.

TIPS FOR YOU! Talk to your parents about taking an online or classroom course to learn a new language. Flying around the world like Bessie requires talking to all kinds of people from different places.

Flemmie Pansy KITTRELL

{ 1904–1980 }

Flemmie Pansy Kittrell transformed the public's understanding of nutrition and early childhood development. Graduating from a doctoral program in nutrition at Cornell University in 1936, Flemmie became the first African-American woman to earn such an advanced degree from the university. She was also the first African-American woman to receive a PhD in nutrition from any school. Her research identified proteins and other dietary elements necessary for healthy bodies. She taught her findings to people in India, Japan, West Africa, Central Africa, Guinea, and Russia. Her 50-year career reshaped approaches to meeting children's nutritional needs and helped establish scientific standards for battling hunger.

A gift to her parents—and to the many lives she eventually changed—Flemmie was born in Henderson, North Carolina, on Christmas Day in 1904. She was the eighth of nine children. Her great-grandparents had been enslaved. To push their children beyond the limits of the family's humble beginnings, her mother and father, Alice and James, encouraged them to study. At the time, many African-American families needed their children to help bring in the meager earnings they made from fieldwork. Flemmie's parents, however, allowed her to attend school. That was a good thing because Flemmie liked studying much more than farming.

She was excited about the chance to read and explore new ideas. She reflected, "I remember very well my first year in school. I had a very good teacher. She was so good and so pretty, that when I was promoted to the second grade, I cried. It was really that teacher who gave me my great love for school." Flemmie's enthusiasm for learning continued, and so did her parents' support. Her father would read poems to his children, enhancing their vocabulary and ability to retain information.

Soon, she was on track to graduate high school at Hampton Academy. However, she found herself unable to pay for the final year. The academy, attached to Hampton Institute (now University), allowed students to complete a "work-year," during which they did chores to pay for their tuition. This kind of labor exchange was made famous by Hampton's most well-known student, Booker T. Washington, who became president of Tuskegee Institute (now Tuskegee University) in Alabama. Once Flemmie had saved enough from her work-year, she graduated—not surprisingly—with honors.

She advanced to the college level at Hampton Institute, where she majored in home economics and focused on ways to improve people's everyday lives. While on campus, she joined the Religious Work Committee and the YWCA. She helped create the Calliope Club and Literary Society. The group, like her beloved father, promoted the language arts. She and some classmates also ran a tearoom, providing tasty drinks, ice cream, sandwiches, salads, and cakes to students, faculty, and campus visitors.

Flemmie also joined the Home Economics Association. This group organized events such as "Baby Day," which allowed tired mothers from surrounding communities to enjoy some alone time while volunteers cared for their children and took them to the beach. Students connected to the association also developed and managed playgrounds, children's activities, and gardening projects. Noticing her bright mind and leadership skills, Flemmie's professors encouraged her to enroll in graduate school.

College broadened Flemmie's perspective. Some of her classmates came from other states or even other parts of the world, such as Africa, the Virgin Islands, and Puerto Rico. On top of that, the 1920s were an exciting time for women entering college and professional schools. Women were beginning to defy the expectation that they would stay at home rather than pursue higher education. Flemmie nervously accepted a scholarship to Cornell University in New York. She finished her master's degree in 1930 and her PhD in nutrition in 1936.

Flemmie's father died from a hernia, and her sister from a vitamin deficiency. These losses made her especially concerned about the science of physical health. Her research focused on average homes in African-American communities. She interviewed women in Greensboro, North Carolina, about prenatal care, medical access, the delivery of their infants, and their plans for feeding their children. She kept careful records and detailed charts of the data she collected. Her research showed that in a state with already high infant mortality rates, black children were dying at higher rates than white children. She also found that the Great Depression was affecting families' abilities to meet their nutritional needs. That was challenging to begin with because no one had yet developed adequate nutritional standards. She set out to change that.

Flemmie taught at Bennett College for a short time, training students in diet instruction, domestic management, and family care. Later, in 1940, she returned to Hampton University, working as the dean of women and head of the home economics department. She was well known for applying home economics solutions to social problems. Mordecai Johnson, Howard University's first African-American president, learned of Flemmie's reputation for serious teaching and personally requested that she come to the prestigious university in Washington, DC. In 1944, she joined the

"THE FAMILY IS OUR PRIMARY HEALTH EDUCATION AGENCY."

faculty as head of the home economics department and remained there until she retired.

She developed a new curriculum that incorporated science and engineering courses into the home economics program. She also founded Howard University's nursery school. The research she did at Howard played a major part in the creation of national programs, including Head Start, a US Department of Health and Human Services program that serves low-income children and their families to this day. She always believed that child development professionals should take special interest in poor and rural communities.

Flemmie went on a tour to improve nutrition for people around the world. In 1947, she led a group to Liberia, where she conducted tests and found that people's diets did not have enough vitamins or protein. She called this form of malnutrition—characterized by full stomachs without the necessary nutrients—"hidden hunger." In 1950, Flemmie received a Fulbright award to carry out nutritional research in India, where she helped Baroda University in western India start a home economics department. She also studied nutritional habits in Japan, Hawaii, and the Congo, designing a nutrition curriculum for their educational programs as well. Her reports were printed in several professional science journals and led to many changes in farm-to-table practices around the globe.

Flemmie received awards from many universities and organizations, including the National Council of Negro Women's Scroll of Honor and an honorary degree from the University of North Carolina, Greensboro. The Home Economics Association offers a scholarship in her honor. Although she formally retired in 1972, she continued giving talks about the importance of science-backed nutrition until her death from a heart attack at the age of 75. Flemmie is an icon in the field of childhood education and quality diet, which are deeply important to every family.

EXPLORE MORE! Visit https://kidshealth.org for tips about eating healthy and keeping fit.

TIPS FOR YOU! Look for kids' cookbooks at your local library or search for kid-friendly recipes online to make your own healthy snacks or even prepare a simple meal for your family. Make sure to ask a parent before using the oven or sharp utensils.

Mamie Phipps CLARK

{1917–1983}

All children should receive the same learning opportunities. Unfortunately, laws in the United States have allowed some kids to participate in programs that boost their success, while other children are left with second-rate programs that hurt their chances to learn. Some students attend school in safe buildings and have high-quality books and supplies, while others attend schools where they have fewer resources and may be wrongly assumed to be unintelligent.

Mamie Phipps Clark knew this was not right. With her husband's help, she built the Northside Center for Child Development in Harlem, New York, in 1946. This was the first full-time guidance facility for kids. They provided tutoring to children of families who did not have much money and conducted tests that proved that black children who had been mistreated were not "bad" or unintelligent. Through her groundbreaking experiments, Mamie helped change the laws that allowed schools to treat kids unfairly. She provided expert testimony in the *Brown v. Board of Education* Supreme Court case, which decided that separating children in schools based on their race was both unequal and illegal.

Mamie was born into science. Her father, Harold, was a doctor, and her mother, Katie, helped manage his office. On April 18, 1917, in Hot Springs, Arkansas, Mamie's parents welcomed her into what was considered to be a privileged situation for an African-American child. As a doctor and spa hotel owner, Mamie's father could afford to provide nice things for his family and take them on fun trips. Their upper-class status gave them access to certain parts of town usually reserved for whites only. The Great Depression, which devastated so many families, left theirs relatively untouched. Mamie described her childhood as happy and comfortable, but, because of the racism of the era, she still had to attend segregated schools.

Segregation did not break her spirit. Mamie remembered, "I loved school." She earned good grades and won scholarships to two of the most prominent African-American universities in the country: Fisk University in Tennessee and Howard University in Washington, DC. She chose to attend Howard in the nation's lively capital. She had heard of so many notable people, including philosophers, doctors, and lawyers, who taught there. They were her role models.

> **"ALTHOUGH MY HUSBAND HAD EARLIER SECURED A TEACHING POSITION AT THE CITY COLLEGE OF NEW YORK, FOLLOWING MY GRADUATION IT SOON BECAME APPARENT TO ME THAT A BLACK FEMALE WITH A PHD IN PSYCHOLOGY WAS AN UNWANTED ANOMALY IN NEW YORK CITY IN THE EARLY 1940S."**

In 1934, she started college at the young age of 16, hoping one day to make as strong an impact as they had. Majoring in math and physics was no easy task. Mamie had to study more than she ever had. She went to summer school twice in a row to make sure she was up to speed. One summer, she even took five courses.

Unfortunately, the math professors at Howard treated Mamie coldly. They were not known to encourage women, and Mamie was no exception. Mamie met Kenneth Clark, a psychology major, and they developed a friendship. Noticing her frustration, Kenneth suggested that Mamie consider transferring to the psychology department. Professor Francis Cecil Sumner, head of Howard's department of psychology, was the first African American to receive a PhD in the field. Unlike the math faculty, Dr. Sumner supported Mamie's interest. It was an ideal fit. Mamie would soon have the opportunity to combine her longtime enthusiasm for children with her thirst for research. She was grateful to Kenneth for making the suggestion. They became close and decided to marry.

Strong willed and smart, Mamie made decisions for herself. Her parents wanted her to wait until she graduated before marrying Kenneth. Instead, they wed in secret during her senior year of college in 1937. Mamie received her bachelor's degree from Howard, earning top honors. She had done so well that the university awarded her a graduate school fellowship. She immediately began working toward her master's degree. Her thesis investigated how African-American children saw themselves. She specifically examined their awareness of race. She found that children knew they were considered "black" very early in their childhood, around age 4 or 5. These early reports would lead to more, including her famous "doll test."

Things were coming together for Mamie. Still, the inequality that came with segregation always aggravated her. She believed her research could prove that discrimination in education was wrong and that African-American children were just as capable of learning as anyone else. She just needed to connect with the right people who both agreed *and* could do something about it.

In 1938, Mamie was working at the law office of Charles Hamilton Houston, a well-known attorney who focused on civil rights issues. Many influential lawyers and people linked to the National Association for the Advancement of Colored People (NAACP) visited Houston's office. Mamie met most, if not all, of them, including a young Thurgood Marshall, who later became the first African-American Supreme Court justice. Each lawyer was brilliant and dedicated to ending racial inequality. Mamie kept developing her identity tests and collecting data. She and her husband worked together to write scientific articles that communicated how African-American children saw themselves. She called her time in Houston's office a "most marvelous learning experience."

Although she was becoming well known for her work, everything was not perfect. Her primary advisor at Columbia University, where she studied psychology as a graduate student, did not agree with her perspective. He believed segregation should continue. Not having the support of her advisor made her research more difficult. Additionally, some faculty at Columbia disagreed with the conclusions she drew in her dissertation, "Changes in Primary Mental Abilities with Age." Some of the professors wanted to believe that race was the main factor determining whether someone was intelligent. She dealt with these struggles while also raising an infant—her daughter, Kate—and preparing for the birth of her son, Hilton.

In 1943, Mamie graduated from Columbia University with a PhD in psychology. She was the first African-American woman to receive a degree from the school. Although she had earned the highest degree in her field, she still struggled to find a job. She had to face the fact that people did not want to hire a black women in the field of psychology. She described the few jobs she was able to get as humiliating because she was often the only African American and, especially, the only one with a PhD.

Despite these setbacks, Mamie kept going. By now, she had perfected her doll test, which examined how African-American children felt about black and white dolls. The children were asked which doll was "good" and which was "bad." They were also asked which doll looked like them. Many children thought the black doll was bad. Mamie and her husband realized that this was because of the unfair treatment the children experienced in America's prejudiced society. The Clarks found that many of the children who went to segregated schools saw themselves as inferior to white children. Many of those who went to mixed schools expressed more anger about seeing themselves as part of the bad group.

The Clarks were so sad about the children's answers that they delayed publishing the results. More than 10 years after the original tests, NAACP attorneys found out about the couple's findings and asked the Clarks to testify in an important case—*Brown v. Board of Education*—which would decide if segregation in schools would continue. The Clarks' doll test helped the court make its decision. In 1954, the Supreme Court ruled that segregation in public schools was illegal.

Mamie's hard work had paid off. She had made an important achievement in the fight for equality.

It was one of many. Mamie founded the Northside Center in Harlem, New York, to serve children and families. Her goal was to provide the mental health services kids and their parents needed to overcome racism and other forms of discrimination. The center welcomed everyone. She also worked to provide a safe space and re-tested children who had been wrongly labeled as mentally challenged. She argued that many of them were not challenged but simply needed better education and resources.

Using psychology to address issues of injustice was Mamie's dream come true. She was appointed to the board of trustees of several organizations, including Columbia University, Mount Sinai Medical Center, the New York Public Library, the Museum of Modern Art, and the American Broadcasting Company. Mamie provided mental health care services and directed the Northside Center until her retirement in 1979.

EXPLORE MORE! Visit www.northsidecenter.org to learn more about the Northside Center.

TIPS FOR YOU! Do you own any dolls or action figures? Count how many are black, Asian, Latino, or other. How do you feel about them? Talk about it with a parent or older person.

Katherine JOHNSON

{1918–2020}

Katherine Johnson's passion for math took the United States to the Moon and back. A mathematician and rocket scientist, she studied gravity and motion in space. As a result of her intelligence and dedication, she provided the National Aeronautics and Space Administration (NASA) with the necessary calculations to launch many of its most famous missions successfully, including John Glenn's historic 1962 orbit of Earth. Glenn was the first American to circle the planet. Katherine did all of her work without the help of a computer; in fact, she *was* the computer. NASA did not begin to use computers until after Katherine had already outlined the formulas for many of its flights. And when they did begin to use data processing machines, which were not reliable at the time, they asked Katherine to double-check their work.

Katherine Johnson was born in 1918 in White Sulphur Springs, West Virginia. Her parents, Joshua and Joylette, had four children. Although she was the youngest, she was definitely the math whiz. She remembered doing her homework with her siblings: "Everybody studied at a big table and, after I finished mine, I helped them get theirs." Katherine's mother was a teacher, and her father worked as a lumberman, farmer, and handyman wherever employment was available. Public schools in the county in which they lived rejected African-American students. Katherine's parents knew how important education would be for their children, so they sent them to a school in Institute, West Virginia, on the campus of West Virginia State College.

Katherine performed fantastically, skipping a few grades and jumping ahead of her older brother. She enrolled in high school when she was just 10 years old. By the age of 14, she had graduated and entered West Virginia State College, a Historically Black College. Such schools had always welcomed and provided a safe space for African-American students when other places rejected them. At West Virginia State College, Katherine found a thriving African-American community. She joined Alpha Kappa Alpha, the first black college sorority. Angie Turner King, a mathematician and scientist, saw young Katherine's potential and took her under her wing.

Katherine met another important mentor there—William Schieffelin Claytor, the third African American to receive a doctoral degree in math. He saw just how bright Katherine was and added advanced math classes to the curriculum to help her sharpen her skills. Sometimes, she was the only person enrolled. By the time she graduated summa cum laude in 1937, she had earned two degrees: one in math, and the other in French. She was almost certain she would become a nurse or a teacher because those were the only fields that readily accepted women. She started her career as she thought she would, teaching at a public school in Marion, Virginia.

Bigger opportunities were budding, and the people Katherine met would soon help her snag them. Around this time, Lloyd Gaines graduated from Lincoln University—a black college located in Missouri. Gaines wanted to become an attorney, but because Lincoln did not have a law school, he applied to the University of Missouri's Law School. The University of Missouri denied his application because he was African American. Gaines saw this as a violation of the 14th Amendment and sued. His case made its way to the Supreme Court in *Missouri ex rel. Lloyd Gaines v. Canada*. In 1938, the court ruled that states that provided higher education options to whites must do the same for African Americans.

West Virginia State's president, John Davis, was heavily involved in civil rights issues and wanted to integrate the graduate schools in West Virginia. The recent *Gaines* ruling made 1939 the perfect time. He recommended Katherine and two male African-American students for enrollment in the graduate program at West Virginia University, the state's white

"IT WAS MY JOB. I DID IT CORRECTLY AND WELL."

school. All three were accepted, making them the first blacks in the program. However, Katherine decided to leave after a year to focus on her family with her first husband, James Goble.

Katherine and her husband had three baby girls, Constance, Joylette, and Katherine. Her youngest daughter fondly recalled her mom always putting their family first. The genius mathematician taught her daughters to sew, and she used math to help others. She tutored outside of her work hours, never charging for the service. When her husband became ill, she devoted herself to caring for him until he died in 1956. In 1959, she married a man named James Johnson.

Other changes were on the horizon. During a family gathering, a relative told Katherine about jobs available for math specialists. NASA's Langley Research Center in Hampton, Virginia, often hired African-American professionals who came from Hampton University. Katherine applied and began working in NASA's segregated "colored computers" office.

At that time, "computers" referred to people, not machines. The colored computers were black women who solved complex math problems to help plan future flights and study ones that had already occurred. The women wrote superb reports on their research, but their male supervisors usually got the credit. One of them admitted that Katherine had already done most of the work on one of the reports and suggested she be the one to finish it. The head of the Flight Research Division of NASA reluctantly agreed. "That was the first time a woman in our division had her name on something," Katherine said. Katherine earned a reputation at NASA for being fantastically accurate. She helped write NASA's first textbook on space, and her calculations shaped the era's possibilities in aeronautics. She co-wrote 26 scientific papers and, in 1961, calculated the trajectory for Alan Shepard, the first American in space.

The mastermind relied on more than her skills with numbers. She worked extremely hard to get things done. When President John F. Kennedy announced the goal of sending a man to the Moon, people all over the nation felt a sense of urgency to make it happen. Russians had already sent a spacecraft to the Moon, so the pressure was on for the United States to send people there. Katherine got to NASA early each morning and went home in the late afternoon to check on her daughters. She returned to the office in the evening to continue working on the equations that would get the American astronauts to the Moon. She worked 14 to 16 hours most days.

Finally, on July 16, 1969, the Apollo 11 mission launched three men into outer space as Katherine beamed with pride. She recalled her method: "I computed the path that would get you there. You determined where you were on Earth . . . when you started out, and where the Moon would be at a given time. We told them how fast they would be going and the Moon will be there by the time you got there." Sure enough, on July 20, they landed on the Moon, and, on July 24, they returned home safely by splashing into the Pacific Ocean.

In 1970, NASA's Apollo 13 mission failed because an oxygen tank exploded. The crew, however, returned without harm by following the specific rescue procedures Katherine had charted.

By the time Katherine retired from NASA in 1986, she had worked for the agency more than 30 years. She provided expertise for the official Space Shuttle program as well as key research on humans in Mars in preparation for future missions. The space agency, which once made her use a separate and inconveniently located bathroom because of her race, named a building in her honor: The Katherine G. Johnson Computational Research Facility. It sits on the site of NASA's campus in Hampton, Virginia.

Inspired by her work, toy brands Barbie and Lego developed figures designed to inspire children to learn science.

In 2015, President Barack Obama awarded Katherine Johnson the Presidential Medal of Freedom.

The following year, the Hollywood movie *Hidden Figures*, about Katherine's and other women's achievements at NASA, was released in theaters. Katherine remained humble about her contributions to science. She sang in her local church choir for 50 years during and after her time with NASA.

EXPLORE MORE! To learn more about Katherine Johnson and the other "human computers" at NASA, look for *Hidden Figures Young Readers' Edition* at your local library.

TIPS FOR YOU! "I counted everything [as a youngster]. I counted the steps to the road, the steps up to church, the number of dishes and silverware I washed . . . anything that could be counted, I did." What's something you do well and often? Talk to a parent about how you might one day build a career doing this!

Jane Cooke WRIGHT

{ 1919–2013 }

Jane Cooke Wright was born into a family of medical history makers. It is no surprise, then, that Jane grew up to make history on her own by developing treatment options for cancer patients. She was one of the first scientists to conduct cancer research using human tissue rather than tissue from mice. Doing so led to major discoveries in identifying the best medications for killing certain types of cancers. Her achievements in cancer research directly led to the decline of the disease in those suffering from leukemia, lymphoma, and sarcoma. Skin cancer and breast cancer treatments improved as well because of the studies she spearheaded. She also invented ways to get chemotherapy to exact places in the body so it would not destroy other parts. People familiar with her groundbreaking work call Jane the "Godmother of Chemotherapy."

Her family's remarkable medical legacy began with her grandfather, Ceah Ketcham Wright. He was born into slavery but graduated as a member of one of the earliest classes of Meharry Medical College—the first medical school in the South for African Americans. His son, Louis Tompkins Wright, graduated from Clark Atlanta University, also a school for blacks, before going on to complete medical school at the prestigious Harvard University. He was the first African American to practice surgery at a nonsegregated hospital in New York. Tompkins Wright married Corinne Cooke, a schoolteacher, and the couple had two daughters: Jane and Barbara.

Jane was born in New York City in 1919. Because her mother was a schoolteacher, learning was a priority in the home. On top of that, New York was in the midst of the Harlem Renaissance, an explosion of black intellectual, social, and cultural expression. Some of the world's greatest novelists, poets, singers, dancers, visual artists, and composers resided there. Jane loved reading and watercolor painting. She had fun swimming and sailing, too.

Her family survived the financial hardships of the Great Depression, and she graduated high school in 1938. She enrolled at Smith College in Massachusetts, where she began to pursue a degree in art. However, her father convinced her to focus on pre-medicine classes. It did not take long for her family's smarts to show up in her performance as a student in her new major. She quickly earned a full scholarship to New York Medical College.

A hard worker and focused student, Jane graduated in three years from a fast-track program. After she left medical school, she worked an internship for two years. During that time, she married attorney David Jones and, later, raised two daughters who admired her work ethic. One said, "She never gives up and never sees the 'no' in anything." Jane balanced her work with her dedication to her family. She once stated, "My plans for the future are to continue seeking a cure for cancer, to be a good mother to my children, and a good wife to my husband."

In 1949, Jane worked with the person who had been most influential to her career: her father. She went to work with him at the Cancer Research Foundation he founded at Harlem Hospital. The two made a fantastic team. They both had scientific expertise and a desire to help as many people as possible. Their family bond almost certainly made their time in the lab more productive. At the time, chemotherapy—mostly known as a radiation procedure—was new and usually only performed at the latest stage of cancer. It was not a well-understood solution. Most doctors viewed surgery as the only dependable treatment. The father-daughter team began testing chemicals known as folic acid antagonists on solid tumors in research trials. Many of their patients saw their tumors shrink under this innovative treatment. Their findings helped establish methotrexate as a beneficial medication. It is still one of the main chemotherapy remedies used today.

"THE ULTIMATE GOAL WAS TO BRING INTO THE SPECIALTY 'A GREATER NUMBER OF TALENTED INDIVIDUALS WHO SHARED THE GOAL OF WINNING THE BATTLE AGAINST THE RAVAGES OF CANCER.'"

Their success boosted their determination to do even more. Jane developed ways to administer multiple medicines at once so patients could heal faster and avoid getting sicker from taking different medicines separately. She successfully identified treatments for breast and skin cancer, increasing the average lifespan of cancer victims by about 10 years.

She also designed techniques to help patients avoid surgery completely. By using a catheter, or a narrow tube inserted through a small incision in the body, she could deliver cancer-killing medications to tumors deep inside the body without the need for major, and possibly life-threatening, surgery.

She published more than 100 papers on her discoveries and shared her new treatment ideas with other influential doctors. In fact, she helped organize a group of specialists so they could all share the best new practices for caring for those with cancer. The group became known as the American Society of Clinical Oncology (ASCO).

When Jane's father died in 1952, she took his place as head of the Cancer Research Foundation at Harlem

Hospital. She was just 33 years of age. When performing surgery, she removed tumors and saved them for testing in her lab. She continued to determine which agents worked best for killing various kinds of cancers by using human tissue to run tests. She took her work abroad, seeing patients in Ghana, Kenya, Europe, China, and the Soviet Union. Back in New York, she joined the New York University Medical Center as an associate professor of surgical research and director of cancer chemotherapy research.

In 1964, President Lyndon B. Johnson chose Dr. Wright to contribute to the President's Commission on Heart Disease, Cancer, and Stroke. The commission's research provided the necessary information to establish treatment centers around the nation. President Johnson selected her, once more, to serve on the National Cancer Advisory Board, and, in 1971, she became the first woman elected president of the New York Cancer Society. She served as vice president of the African Medical and Research Foundation for 11 years, from 1973 to 1984.

EXPLORE MORE! Learn about Dr. Hadiyah-Nicole Green, another black pioneer in the area of cancer treatment, at https://weareoralee.org/drgreen/.

TIPS FOR YOU! Research your own family tree and discover how many of your relatives accomplished cool things.

Margaret Strickland COLLINS

{ 1922–1996 }

Have you ever seen insects on display at a museum? If you have, chances are Margaret Strickland Collins had something to do with it. Margaret was an entomologist and considered the foremost expert in termites. She pioneered international research on termite species, including how different types of termites behave and react to other bugs and to various climates and chemicals. Her astonishing knowledge of insects earned her the nickname the "Termite Lady," as well as her position as a longtime curator of the termite collection at the Smithsonian's National Museum of Natural History in Washington, DC. When Margaret earned her doctoral degree from the University of Chicago in 1950, she became the first female African-American entomologist and the third female African-American zoologist.

On September 4, 1922, Margaret Collins was born in Institute, West Virginia. Her parents, Rollins and Luella James, instilled the importance of education into Margaret and her four siblings. Her mother was an avid reader, and her father received an undergraduate degree from West Virginia State College and a master's degree from Tuskegee Institute. In fact, while he was at Tuskegee, her father worked with the famous scientist and inventor George Washington Carver.

Her father eventually returned to Institute and taught agriculture at West Virginia State. There, he headed the poultry program and taught biology at the high school housed within the college. Institute was an all-black town with the college as its main hub, so the community tended to be well educated and sophisticated. Margaret absorbed ideas and vocabulary quickly as she listened to her parents read aloud to her and her siblings. She recalled, "My parents collected an impressive library for their income level." At the age of 6, she began to check out books from the college library. This early exposure to reading sparked her curiosity. When her mother became ill, Margaret started to spend time playing in the woods. The critters she encountered fascinated her young mind.

Finding creepy-crawly insects thrilled little Margaret so much she began to take them home. Her father noticed and challenged her to identify them in books. She had access to all kinds of books on natural history because her dad worked at the college. Neighbors also let her borrow books from their home libraries. The books contained both English and Latin names for the bugs she loved. This early learning shaped her education. She skipped several grades early on and started

"BECAUSE OF MY FAMILY AND MY COMMUNITY, MY CHILDHOOD WAS UNIQUE. I NEVER LEARNED WHAT I COULDN'T DO—AS A CHILD, AS A WOMAN, OR AS A BLACK PERSON."

high school at age 11. Margaret did not always fit in because she was much younger than her classmates and, sometimes, the only girl in a class; she later said this helped make her stronger. Though making friends was difficult, she continued to do well in biology and physics. She credited her academic success to fun experiments with the science club and to the great teachers who mentored her. She completed high school in 1937 before she turned 15.

Margaret started college on scholarship at West Virginia State, but her first year did not go so well. She said a boring professor dwindled her interest in science. Her grades suffered, and she lost the scholarship. Now she had to figure out how to pay for school. She worked as a maid to come up with the money and used her free time searching for critters at the nearby Kanawha River.

One day, she spotted a river animal she had never seen before. Her excitement led her to collect samples and share them with a biology professor at the college. The professor, Toye George Davis, was a renowned biologist with a PhD from Harvard University. He was unable to identify the sample immediately, so they sent it to a special lab in Massachusetts. While they awaited the results, Davis gave Margaret a microscope and showed her how to use a taxonomic key. He also gave her a job as a lab assistant and provided her with one of her favorite things: new books. The funny-looking animal turned out to be bryozoan—a type of moss or filter feeder.

Margaret graduated with a degree in biology and minors in physics and German in 1943. Just one year before, Margaret had married Bernard Strickland, a pre-medical student at Howard University. But World War II made this a difficult time; both Margaret's husband and Davis, her beloved teacher, had been drafted into the military. Despite these circumstances, she enrolled in graduate school at the University of Chicago. She wanted to take biology and ecology classes to help her start a business collecting marine life and selling it to biological supply houses. An advisor in the registrar's office tried to discourage her from this goal, but she persisted and ended up taking classes from the great zoologist Alfred E. Emerson.

Emerson was a legendary scholar on termites; he maintained the largest collection of the bug and archive of books on the subject. Although he felt women had too many issues to deal with while doing field research, he decided to give Collins a chance. He could not say "no" to someone so smart and who was as captivated by insects as he was. And Margaret refused to let his thoughts on women prevent her from learning from him. She used his collection to complete her thesis.

In her field notes, Margaret admired the termite's ability to digest wood and explained how termites are good for nature. She reported, "They recycle nutrients, clear up organic debris (rotting limbs and leaves), and create hollowed spaces that other animals might call home." She also wrote about their interesting social structures. They have societies with various roles like soldiers, workers, and queens. "Termites build complex nests using a mixture of mud, feces, and saliva." She called what they built a "sophisticated engineering structure."

When she earned her PhD, Margaret became the first African-American female entomologist and the third black female zoologist in the country. Afterward, she earned a position as an assistant professor at Howard University, where she had followed her first husband to medical school after the war. Unfortunately, Howard's support of female faculty members was low. The institution tended to avoid promoting women quickly and urged them not to wear pants. In 1952, Margaret divorced her husband and decided to take her talents to Florida Agricultural and Mechanical University (FAMU).

Her time at FAMU, a distinguished Historically Black College, brought new opportunities. There, she was named a full professor and chair of her department.

She married Herbert Collins and had two sons. The family often took trips to the Everglades to collect biological samples. She was also involved in civil rights and human equality issues. The enlightened African-American community of Tallahassee inspired Margaret to participate in social justice demonstrations. When the FAMU Student Council called for a bus boycott in the city in May 1956, she drove people to and from work. The police were unhappy with the protest and chased her car. Still, the pressure African Americans placed on city officials forced them to integrate the buses by January 1957. Racial justice issues continued to influence the era. In 1964, the 24th Amendment made the poll tax illegal, and President Lyndon B. Johnson signed the Civil Rights Act, outlawing discrimination in jobs, schools, voting, and public accommodations.

That year, Margaret returned to Washington, DC, and to Howard as a full professor. The Smithsonian appointed her as a research associate, and she guided students on international expeditions. She traveled to Mexico, Belize, Dominica, Guyana, and the British Virgin Islands, collecting and studying termites. Her team collected nearly 13,000 different termite species. She identified their defense mechanisms and developed techniques for controlling termite populations. In 1979, she rebuilt a research station in Guyana named in honor of her old friend and mentor, Alfred Emerson.

With so many experiences, Margaret began to combine her scientific work with her commitment to civil rights. She addressed an audience at the American Association for the Advancement of Science in 1982. Her talk was titled "Science and the Question of Human Equality," and it challenged fake science that said people's race determined their value.

In 1983, Margaret retired from Howard but continued to do what she loved, just as she had when she was a little girl at the river. She continued her field trips, examining critters in tropical places. She sent her notes back to the Smithsonian. The National Museum of Natural History named the countless insects she collected and her expert notes The Collins Collection. After a 50-year career, the "Termite Lady" died in the Cayman Islands doing what she loved most—studying small creatures.

EXPLORE MORE! Make a bug hotel! Put an empty container on its side outside and fill it with grass, dirt, and other natural items. Check back often to observe your buggy guests.

TIPS FOR YOU! Margaret Strickland Collins said, "Perhaps the biggest influence of all was contact with individuals who found the discipline of biology fulfilling—enthusiasm sometimes behaves as an infectious agent."

Do you have a friend or family member who has an interesting hobby or job? Ask them about it. You might like to try it out too.

Gladys WEST

{1930– }

In one way or another, global positioning systems, or GPS, are part of most people's lives. GPS guides car rides, determines internet search results, affects social media trends, and helps planes land safely. GPS technology was developed by a team of mathematicians who studied Earth's geometric shape and its specific placement in the universe. Gladys West contributed to this team by coding and programming satellite data for engineers at the US Navy Base in Virginia. She calculated formulas involving gravity, radar, and the planet's dimensions. This research established modern GPS.

Gladys West was born in 1930 during the Great Depression in Dinwiddie County, Virginia. As a child, she did farm work in the hot sun. Many African-American families in the rural town made their living sharecropping. This meant they picked cotton, corn, or tobacco on soil they did not own and shared the profits with the landowners. The other option was to work in a tobacco factory. Although her family owned their land, neither farm nor factory labor sounded like much fun to Gladys, who disliked working from sun up to sun down. She wanted to live a different kind of life and promised herself to put school first. She said, "I realized I had to get an education to get out." So, she set out to do just that.

"I made good grades in all of my subjects," she proudly remembered. Growing up in a segregated community motivated her to work hard in school. There were separate schools for black and white children, and black children were often given old textbooks that had already been used in the white schools. These realities pushed Gladys to work harder to accomplish her goal of leaving farm life behind. She graduated at the top of her high school class and received a full scholarship to Virginia State University.

Gladys said, "When it was time to go to college, I didn't quite know what to major in." Since she did well in every subject, people encouraged her to choose something challenging. Gladys chose math. The department was mostly male, and Gladys had to prove she could keep up. She said it felt "different," not quite as inviting and comfortable as the home economics classes filled with young women. Many of the women at her college became teachers, as was expected. Gladys taught, too, for a time after she graduated, but her math degree opened doors beyond the classroom.

In 1956, Gladys joined the Naval Surface Warfare Center's Dahlgren Division, where she was the second black woman ever hired. There were only four African-American employees in total, and two were men. One was Ira West; he and Gladys soon fell in love and married, but neither let their relationship distract them from their responsibilities.

Gladys worked on an important astronomical project that determined Pluto's motion in relation to Neptune. She entered the data into giant supercomputers. She was also tasked with checking these supercomputers' calculations, which were sometimes incorrect. Her reputation for accuracy and attention to detail made its way to her supervisor, Ralph Neiman. He recommended Gladys as project manager for the Seasat radar altimetry project. Seasat was the first satellite that could remotely sense oceans using a special kind of radar.

Gladys felt pressure to do things perfectly because there were so few African Americans and women at the naval facility. The civil rights movement was unfolding at the same time, and women activists—such as Fannie Lou Hamer, Dorothy Cotton, Diane Nash, and Mary McLeod Bethune—were calling for equality. Gladys felt it was not safe for African Americans who worked for the government to be directly involved in the movement. Still, she felt the need to carry the load of "always doing things just right, to set an example for other people who were coming behind." She spent days and nights determining exact satellite calculations.

"BEFORE, YOU SORT OF WHISPERED AND LOOKED AT EACH OTHER, OR SOMETHING, BUT NOW THE WORLD IS OPENING UP A LITTLE BIT AND MAKING IT EASIER FOR WOMEN. BUT THEY STILL GOTTA FIGHT."

Gladys produced an official 60-page illustrated guide for the naval center titled *Data Processing System Specifications for the Geosat Satellite Radar Altimeter*. The guide explained her work on using radar to measure the size and shape of Earth and contributing to the accuracy of GPS. The data she collected and processed from satellites helped establish exact locations all over the globe. She worked at the naval center for 42 years, retiring in 1998 at the age of 68, and later decided to pursue a PhD at Virginia Polytechnic Institute and State University.

As she got older, Gladys had health problems, including a stroke and a breast cancer diagnosis. Her sickness made completing her degree difficult, but she did not let her circumstances defeat her. She said later, "All of a sudden these words came into my head: 'You can't stay in the bed, you've got to get up from here and get your PhD.'" She finished in 2018.

Gladys has remained an active participant in the service work of her sorority, Alpha Kappa Alpha, throughout her life. During one of their meetings, the members learned of Gladys's role in developing GPS when her biography was read aloud. Since then, the organization has helped make the public aware of this pioneer. In December 2018, the United States Air Force inducted West into the Space and Missile Pioneers Hall of Fame during a ceremony at the Pentagon.

EXPLORE MORE! Search for "Navy Hidden Hero: Gladys Mae West and GPS" on YouTube to listen to Gladys talk.

TIPS FOR YOU! Using colored pencils and paper, create a map of your home or neighborhood.

Annie J. EASLEY

{ 1933–2011 }

You may have heard the phrase, "It doesn't take a rocket scientist." Well, if you have, you understand that most day-to-day tasks don't require extreme levels of intelligence to complete. However, to work at NASA as a software developer for launch vehicles, it does, indeed, take a rocket scientist. Annie J. Easley stepped into the role and soared. Annie was a leading member of the team that designed Centaur—the nation's first high-energy, upper stage launch vehicle. Most rockets burn kerosene-based hydrocarbon fuels, but Centaur uses a liquid-hydrogen/liquid-oxygen recipe. The special concoction produces a greater thrust and the ability to carry more cargo into space. Annie's important contributions to the team as a mathematician and computer engineer helped make the machine more efficient.

Annie was born on April 23, 1933, in Birmingham, Alabama—also called "Bombingham" because of the many times it was bombed by white supremacists targeting African Americans. She was raised by her mother, Mary. The city could be a scary place for African-American children, and her family did not have a lot of money. Annie did not let those circumstances hold her back. She did well throughout school. Annie credited her mother for her success as a child and described her mother as her "biggest cheerleader."

Annie graduated as valedictorian of her high school class and began to think about her career options. Girls were usually pushed into teaching or nursing at the time, but she had no interest in either. Pharmacy (the study of the uses and effects of drugs) sounded more interesting to her. She left Birmingham to major in pharmacy at Xavier University, a Historically Black College in New Orleans, Louisiana.

After two years in New Orleans, Annie left school and returned to Birmingham with a new military husband. She took a job as a substitute teacher. Unfortunately, the city's old racist laws and violence were still there. Voting officials made African Americans take difficult, unfair literacy tests to keep them from voting.

Annie's college education gave her an edge, and she helped other African Americans prepare for the tests so they could register to vote. Like many African Americans who were tired of the racial terrorism in the South, Annie and her husband headed north once he was discharged from the military. They settled in Cleveland, Ohio, to be near his family. Annie wanted to return to school to complete her degree in pharmacy, but there were no programs she could attend in the area.

"IF THERE WAS AN 'A' AND A 'B,' SHE WOULD ENCOURAGE ME TO BRING THAT 'B' UP THE NEXT TIME. YOU KNOW, YOU HAVE TO WORK ON THAT. AND I DIDN'T GET PAID. I DIDN'T GET PENNIES OR NICKELS OR QUARTERS FOR GRADES. WELL, I KNOW SOME FAMILIES DO THAT. I DIDN'T GET THAT KIND—IT WAS NOT THAT KIND OF THING. IT WAS HER ENCOURAGEMENT, HER PLEASURE, AND HER SMILE, WHEN THE REPORT CARD CAME HOME."

In 1955, she happened to read an interesting newspaper article about twin sisters who worked as "human computers" at NACA (the National Advisory Committee for Aeronautics, later known as NASA). She was in the right place at the right time. One of NACA's main research headquarters was in Cleveland. Annie applied and, two weeks later, found herself putting her math genius to use for the space agency.

Annie performed complex mathematical calculations for the engineering team in the Computer Services Division. She was not intimidated by the job. She said the encouragement her mother gave her as a girl had boosted her self-esteem. "I already had my belief in myself when I came here," she recalled. She was one of only four African Americans among the agency's 2,500 employees.

“I’M OUT HERE TO GET THE JOB DONE, AND I KNEW I HAD THE ABILITY TO DO IT, AND THAT’S WHERE MY FOCUS WAS.”

Despite her good work, racism followed her everywhere. When a group photo of the “human computer” team was put on display at a special event at the center, her face was cut out of the picture. She took it in stride, saying, “I’m out here to do a job and I knew I had the ability to do it, and that’s where my focus was, on getting the job done. I was not intentionally trying to be a pioneer.”

Later during her time at NASA, Annie began working on nuclear-powered rocket systems, including the Centaur—a high-energy booster rocket that first launched successfully in 1963. Nicknamed NASA’s “workhorse in space,” it was used to send communications, weather information, military satellites, and other space vehicles into space.

Sometimes, Annie traveled to the launch site in Florida to observe the flights. The Centaur rocket measured 30 feet in length and 10 feet in diameter. It weighed more than 35,000 pounds when fueled and could carry as much as 5,000 pounds of cargo. By the 1970s, Centaur served as the upper stage rocket for visits to other planets, including Mercury, Venus, Mars, Jupiter, Saturn, Uranus, and Neptune. Centaur also supported projects created to explore space beyond the Sun's solar system.

In addition to her work on rockets, Annie contributed to major research on the ozone layer, solar wind, and solar energy. One project she worked on helped determine the capacity of battery power in electric cars, which laid the groundwork for hybrid car technology. During her 32 years at NASA, she also completed her bachelor's degree in math at Cleveland State University, paying for her courses on her own.

She also took advanced classes from NASA in Houston to prepare for specialty work at the agency. She served as an equal employment opportunity officer at the agency as well, investigating and helping resolve issues related to discrimination. The longtime rocket scientist also traveled to colleges and universities to recruit engineers for NASA. She established and led the first ski club at NASA's Lewis Research Center (now Glenn Research Center) and tutored children and dropouts returning to school. Despite her many accomplishments at the organization, she retired in 1989 without ever receiving a promotion from NASA.

EXPLORE MORE! Visit www.nasa.gov/kidsclub to learn more about scientists like Annie.

TIPS FOR YOU! Did you know you can see some planets without a telescope? Look for *Astronomy for Kids* at the library to learn more.

Patricia BATH

{ 1942–2019 }

If restoring sight to the blind is a miracle, then Dr. Patricia Bath was a miracle worker: She did exactly that for several people who had been blind for decades. Patricia restored sight by implanting an artificial cornea, called a keratoprosthesis, into the person's eye. The pioneering medical scientist and ophthalmologist also invented a device called the laserphaco probe, which is used to treat cataracts—an eye condition that causes blurry vision and can lead to blindness. Patricia's invention was more precise, less dangerous, and easier on patients than previous surgical treatments for the condition. She received a patent allowing her to make and sell the device in 1988, which made her the first African-American doctor awarded a medical patent. She also founded the nonprofit American Institute for the Prevention of Blindness in Washington, DC. Patricia committed her career to preventing, treating, and curing blindness. Years of hard work, beginning in her childhood, led to her success.

Patricia was born on November 4, 1942, in Harlem, New York. Her parents, Rupert and Gladys, were working-class people. Rupert emigrated from Trinidad to the United States and worked as a train operator for the New York subway system. Gladys was a descendent of African slaves and did domestic work. They emphasized the importance of education to their two children. Patricia and her brother both excelled in math and science.

By the time Patricia had reached high school, she was selected as a National Science Foundation scholar. As a result, she contributed to a major research project at Harlem Hospital, establishing the relationships between cancer, nutrition, and stress, which earned her a front-page feature in the *New York Times*. Her early accomplishments ignited both excitement and pride in herself. She remembered, "I was in Harlem, it was the tip of the civil rights era, I think that was noteworthy, that a black child in Harlem could be doing scientific research alongside a white kid from the Hamptons."

Her path from young student to groundbreaking doctor continued to be marked by awards and honors. Her findings from the National Science Foundation cancer project impressed the public, and *Mademoiselle* magazine issued her a recognition of merit. Patricia and her brother graduated from Charles Evans High School, and, afterward, she remained in New York to obtain her bachelor's degree in chemistry at Hunter College. After graduating from Hunter, she moved to

"I HAD A FEW OBSTACLES BUT I HAD TO SHAKE IT OFF."

Washington, DC, and began her studies at Howard University's College of Medicine.

Howard's long history of producing well-known doctors fostered its reputation as the top choice for young African-American medical students. For instance, Dr. Charles Drew, who organized the first large-scale blood bank in the United States, was an instructor and chief surgical resident at Howard's Freedmen's Hospital. The school's reputation and its demanding professors left little room for students to perform poorly. Patricia made good grades in all her classes and even received a National Government Fellowship Award to conduct research in (the former) Yugoslavia. There, she got a chance to meet Earl Warren, a US Supreme Court justice. She graduated with honors in 1968, earning the Edwin J. Watson Prize for Outstanding Student in Ophthalmology.

Unfortunately, racial tensions dating back to slavery led to continued conflict in the United States. Martin Luther King Jr. was killed the year Patricia finished medical school. Inspired by his example, Patricia, at the age of 26, joined the Poor People's Campaign, which

Dr. King had organized to address inequalities that led to poverty. Patricia was familiar with that struggle from her upbringing in Harlem. Blacks had far fewer career and educational opportunities than whites. Her mother scrubbed floors so Patricia could go to medical school. Following King's assassination, Patricia organized Howard University medical students on a volunteer mission to provide health care services to the Poor People's Campaign in Resurrection City in the summer of 1968.

Patricia soon returned to her Harlem community to intern at Harlem Hospital Center. While there, she continued to advocate for equality and civil rights. She researched the conditions of blind patients at Harlem Hospital as compared to those at the Columbia University Eye Clinic. Harlem Hospital Center had no ophthalmology staff or department, and the black Harlem patients had little money. As a result, the patients were receiving substandard care. Patricia convinced surgeons at Columbia to provide services to Harlem patients free of charge. She also organized volunteer initiatives that provided free eyeglasses to children whose families could not afford them.

In 1969, Patricia proudly participated on the team that performed the first eye surgery at Harlem Hospital. She also completed a transplant fellowship, during which she mastered replacing the human cornea with an artificial one. She finished her training at New York University from 1970 to 1973, where she was the first African-American resident in ophthalmology. Amid accomplishing so much, she also became a mother, giving birth to a baby girl in 1972.

In 1974, Patricia became an assistant professor of surgery at Charles R. Drew University and an assistant professor of ophthalmology at the University of California, Los Angeles (UCLA). The following year, she became the first female faculty member in the department of ophthalmology at UCLA's Jules Stein Eye Institute. She was offered an office "in the basement, next to the lab animals." She refused the spot. "I didn't say it was racist or sexist. I said it was inappropriate and succeeded in getting acceptable office space. I decided I was just going to do my work." By 1983, she was the chair of the ophthalmology residency program at Drew-UCLA and the first woman in the United States to hold such a position.

Patricia was concerned with preventable causes of blindness, particularly among minority communities. She found that African Americans were nearly twice as likely to go blind from glaucoma as non-blacks in the United States. But she was also concerned about people outside the States who weren't getting the treatment they needed.

As the director of the American Institute for the Prevention of Blindness, Patricia traveled widely. She worked with the Laser Medical Center of Berlin in West Germany, the Rothschild Eye Institute of Paris in France, and the Loughborough Institute of Technology in England. On these travels, she performed corneal transplants, taught new medical techniques, donated equipment, lectured, met with colleagues, and witnessed the disparity in health services available in industrial and developing countries.

Patricia's interest, experience, and research on cataracts led to her invention of a new device and method to remove cataracts: the laserphaco probe. When she first conceived of the device in 1981, her idea was more advanced than other technologies available at the time. It took her nearly five years to complete the research and testing needed to make it work. Today, the device is used around the world to restore sight to those with cataracts.

After her retirement in 1993, Patricia became an advocate of telemedicine—the use of electronic communication to provide medical services to areas where health care is limited. Her greatest passion, however, continued to be fighting blindness. "The ability to restore sight is the ultimate reward," she said.

EXPLORE MORE! Visit www.thehistorymakers.org and search "Patricia Bath" to see a video of Patricia talking about her work.

TIPS FOR YOU! Learn more about blindness and what is being done to help people with vision impairment at www.blindnessprevention.org.

Alexa Irene CANADY

{1950– }

In 1981, Alexa Irene Canady became the first African-American woman neurosurgeon in the United States. Alexa served as chief of neurosurgery at Children's Hospital of Michigan for 14 years. During her time in that position, she focused on helping children with genetic spine problems, head injuries, and brain tumors. She also provided treatment to children suffering from dangerous conditions that caused their brains to fill with excess fluid. Her own challenges as a youth, her kind heart, and her commitment to curing young people guided her journey.

Alexa was born in Lansing, Michigan. Her parents, Elizabeth and Clinton, attended Fisk University, a Historically Black College in Nashville, Tennessee, where they met and fell in love. They married just before Clinton began his military service during World War II. After returning from war, he moved the family to the manufacturing town of Lansing, Michigan, where he worked as a dentist. Alexa's mother

"IF YOU DO GOOD WORK, THE REST DOESN'T MATTER."

was a former national president of the Delta Sigma Theta sorority, a prestigious organization for educated African-American women.

Alexa remembered growing up in the 1950s, when girls were expected to dress "appropriately." She regularly wore white gloves, hats, and stockings. She also recalled what it was like to exist in a mostly segregated world. "My brother and I stuck out as the only black kids at our rural elementary school," she said. However, their mother reminded them that no one had the right to make them feel uncomfortable or as if they didn't deserve to be there. Alexa explained, "My mother frequently gave us her famous 'tokens are for spending' talk. She said, 'Let them make you the token—so what if you're the token black girl. Take that token and spend it.'"

Her mother's encouragement and the time spent with her grandmother shaped some of Alexa's earliest experiences. After she completed second grade, her grandmother came to stay with their family during the summer. Her grandmother was a schoolteacher taking a course in mental testing at a local college. She included Alexa in some of the experiments. Alexa scored so well on one particular exam that her grandmother's professor requested that Alexa take additional tests. Alexa remembered, "I sat at a desk at the front of the classroom while her professor showed me pictures and numbers and asked me questions until my brain felt numb." A week later, the professor called their home to tell Alexa's parents that her intelligence level was "off the charts." They found that odd, given her average scores at school. They eventually discovered that Alexa's teacher had been dishonest about her performance, switching her scores with those of a white girl in the class.

Alexa's excellent academic record led her to study math at the University of Michigan. At first she doubted herself, but came across a scholarship opportunity that prompted her to give college a try. She received a degree in zoology in 1971. However, she had spent some time in a genetics lab during her studies and attended a genetic counseling clinic. As a result, she fell in love with human medicine. So, instead of pursuing a career in zoology, she transitioned to the University of Michigan's Medical School.

There were about 25 women in her class of 200. Five or six were African Americans. She reflected, "It quickly became apparent that we were in a man's world." Professors often ignored women with raised hands in class. Most of the prominent campus clubs and societies were for men only. The white women in her class were outraged that they weren't being taken as seriously as the men, but Alexa was used to discrimination. "I just put my head down and worked harder. I was used to being disregarded," she said.

During her first two years of medical school, Alexa became excited by neurology—the branch of medicine dealing with the nerves and nervous system—and by the human brain, which, to her, was the most mysterious and intriguing organ in the human body. She described the unforgettable first time she observed a surgeon open a human skull. "I watched, mesmerized, as he traversed the brain, his tools steering gracefully through delicate tissues and over tiny nerves and vessels. I was a goner." She realized that neurosurgery was the career for her. She also knew it would be very difficult to join such a heavily male-dominated field. She would have to get into a specialty residency program that only admitted one or two candidates per year.

"I inhaled every publication and article I could get my hands on, and I attended every conference and seminar. I went to meetings and asked questions just to make myself known." Her work paid off; she got a meeting with the chairman of neurosurgery at the university. She arrived jittery and full of excitement, but her excitement soon turned to fright. For two hours, he talked about all the people he had fired from the program, and she soon realized he was interviewing her under pressure and didn't actually want her there. She refused to give up. She continued to interview

> **"SURGERY IS A THOUSAND STEPS. AT FIRST, THEY JUST LET YOU CLOSE THE SKIN. THEN THEY LET YOU OPEN THE SKIN. THEN THEY LET YOU MAKE THE BURR HOLES THAT OPEN UP THE SKULL. YOU GO THROUGH IT STEP BY STEP—ALWAYS ON YOUR TOES, CONSTANTLY LOOKING FOR THE UNEXPECTED . . . IT'S NOT UNCOMMON TO ENCOUNTER SOMETHING THAT MAKES IT IMPOSSIBLE TO CONTINUE AS PLANNED."**

around the country for months. Finally, Yale University accepted her for a surgical internship in 1975.

When she got there, she heard an administrator say, "Oh, you must be our new equal-opportunity package." Alexa remembered her mother's advice not to let anyone make her feel unworthy. She dismissed the bullies and continued her study of the human brain.

Alexa soon began focusing on brain surgery for children. For her, healing kids and giving their families hope was the greatest feeling in the world. She said the work was rewarding because, most of the time, the treatments made the children feel and function better. After the internship, she went to the University of Minnesota, joining the university's neurosurgery department as the first African-American female neurosurgery resident in the country.

Patient care was Alexa's top priority, and her peers appreciated her efforts. She served as a neurosurgery resident at Children's Hospital of Philadelphia from 1981 to 1982, where her fellow doctors voted her one of the top residents. Later, in 1987, she returned to Michigan as chief of neurosurgery at Children's Hospital until she retired in June 2001.

In 1984, the American Board of Neurological Surgery certified Alexa, making her the first African-American female pediatric neurosurgeon. Under her guidance, her department at Children's Hospital became one of the best in the United States. She also taught at Wayne State University while working as a surgeon. At Wayne State, she conducted research that eventually led to the creation of a device to help treat hydrocephalus—a brain condition mainly affecting the very young and the elderly.

Alexa was inducted into the Michigan Women's Hall of Fame. She also received the American Medical Women's Association President's Award. But perhaps her greatest legacy has been caring for thousands of patients with gunshot wounds, brain injuries, and other diseases, and performing complicated life-saving brain and spinal surgeries that have allowed her young patients to look forward to growing up and making their own impact on the lives of others and the world.

After retiring from Children's Hospital in 2001, Alexa moved to Florida but remained active in medicine. She began working part-time at Sacred Heart Hospital in Pensacola after learning there were no surgeons there in her area of specialty. She worked at the hospital until 2012.

EXPLORE MORE! Search "how the body works" at https://kidshealth.org to learn more about the functions of the brain and other parts of the human body.

TIPS FOR YOU! Do you know anyone who went to a Historically Black College, like Alexa did? Ask family and friends to find out.

Mae Carol JEMISON

{1956– }

Who says you have to choose to be good at just *one* thing? Mae Carol Jemison is a dancer, a medical doctor, a teacher, an engineer, and an astronaut. On top of all that, she became the first black woman in the world to go into space when she flew aboard the Space Shuttle *Endeavour* in 1992. She worked at NASA for six years as an astronaut. Her service in the advancement of science and efforts to nurture the interest and inclusion of girls in the field earned her inductions into the National Women's Hall of Fame and the International Space Hall of Fame.

Mae was born October 17, 1956, in Decatur, Alabama. When she was three years old, she and her mother, father, sister, and brother packed their bags and headed to Chicago. Even as a kindergartner, Mae liked exploring. When a teacher asked her what she wanted to be when she grew up, she said she wanted to be a scientist. Her teacher asked, "Did you mean a nurse?"

Little Mae meant what she said. She remained confident and did not second-guess herself, despite reactions like the one from her teacher. "Growing up, I always assumed I would go to space. I wanted to do lots of things. Be a scientist, a dancer, a policymaker," she said. "I would make a difference in what happens in the world, and I knew that I could." She was a problem-solver and wouldn't be intimidated by obstacles. When she got a sore throat as a child, she decided to do a research project on pus. Mae said her parents were the key to her self-confidence and can-do attitude. "They made sure my siblings and I knew about the remarkable contributions that African Americans had made to this world."

As she grew, her interests expanded to include anthropology, archeology, and astrology. She spent hours in the library, soaking up as much information as she could. All that reading paid off. She skipped seventh grade and graduated high school at just 16 years old. She left Morgan Park High in Chicago and went to Stanford University in California on a National Achievement Scholarship in 1973.

At Stanford, Mae double majored in chemical engineering and Afro-American Studies. She remained interested in a number of things. She participated in dance and theater and served as leader of the Black Student Union. She trained in dance and even thought about pursuing it professionally. For a time, she took lessons at the famous Alvin Ailey School of Dance.

"BEING FIRST GIVES YOU A RESPONSIBILITY—YOU HAVE A PUBLIC PLATFORM, AND YOU MUST CHOOSE HOW TO USE IT. I USE MINE TO HELP FOLKS BECOME MORE COMFORTABLE WITH THE IDEA THAT SCIENCE IS INTEGRAL TO OUR WORLD. AND I VOWED THAT I WOULD TALK ABOUT MY WORK AND ASK OTHER WOMEN ABOUT THEIRS—THE NITTY-GRITTY DETAILS."

However, her mother reminded her where to place her focus. She advised, "You can always dance if you're a doctor, but you can't doctor if you're a dancer."

Mae followed her mother's advice. She focused on academics, graduating in 1977 with such an impressive resume and grades that she was accepted into Cornell Medical College. While there, she studied internationally, visiting Cuba, Kenya, and Cambodia on research trips. She received her medical degree in 1981.

Now Mae was ready to work as a physician. She practiced general medicine in the United States for a time before deciding to broaden her horizons. Her studies in African and African-American history and culture turned out to be quite useful. She served as a medical officer for the Peace Corps in Sierra Leone and Liberia for two years. Not only did she care for volunteers and embassy staff, but she also provided support to the Centers for Disease Control and Prevention as a researcher. She wrote self-care manuals and established health and safety guidelines for Peace Corps volunteers.

Once back in the United States, she set her eyes on space. Her fear of heights was not going to stop her from achieving her lifelong dream. She began taking engineering courses while working in a private medical practice before applying to NASA's astronaut program. It was not easy. There were 2,000 applicants and only 15 openings. The stars aligned. In June 1987, on her second try, NASA accepted Mae's application, making her the first African-American woman in the program.

She began training in 1988 at the Kennedy Space Center, where she processed shuttle data and managed flight-related software. By September 1992, it was time to go to space. She boarded NASA's Space Shuttle Endeavour for the shuttle program's 50th mission. Mae conducted experiments on weightlessness and motion sickness during her 190 hours in space and 127 orbits around Earth. Other experiments included making saline water in space, looking at how bone cells responded to a zero-gravity environment, and seeing how tadpoles developed in space.

Besides breaking a major barrier for African-American females by going to space, Mae worked hard to make a positive impact on the world. She left NASA after her flight to launch a company called The Jemison

Group to advise companies about how technological advancements affect society at different levels. Mae also served as an environmental studies professor at Dartmouth College, where she worked on sustainable possibilities in technology for disadvantaged countries, and as a professor-at-large at Cornell University. While teaching, she also founded another company, BioSentient Corporation, to commercialize a technique for controlling motion sickness, which she had experimented with in space.

Hoping to extend opportunities like those she'd had to disadvantaged youths, Mae founded the Dorothy Jemison Foundation for Excellence, named in honor of her mother. The foundation's The Earth We Share (TEWS) program hosts science camps for middle school and high school students around the world. In 2011, she launched the TEWS-Space Race with the goal of improving science achievement for underserved students in Los Angeles. She has also collaborated with large corporations and youth groups to encourage children's interest in the sciences. Mae wrote a memoir intended for children called *Find Where the Wind Goes,* which was published in 2001. In 2013, a four-book collection for children—part of the A True Book series—was published. It included interesting facts about space and concepts from physics and astronomy.

Mae, who was the first real astronaut to appear on the *Star Trek* television series, is leading the 100 Year Starship™ with a grant from the government to create opportunities for human travel beyond the Sun's solar system to another star within the next 100 years. She continues to champion greater inclusion of girls in STEM programs.

EXPLORE MORE! Read *Young, Gifted, and Black: Meet 52 Black Heroes from Past and Present* by Jamia Wilson to learn more about Mae and other influential people in black history.

TIPS FOR YOU! Close your eyes. Imagine you are in space. Write down a list of everything you would take with you and jot a note to family and friends describing what you saw in the galaxy.

Renee GORDON

{ 1984– }

Renee Gordon has built a thriving career in the field of science, technology, engineering, and math (STEM). She is Program Director at Tallahassee Community College in Tallahassee, Florida, where she oversees STEM projects and activities for people of all ages to encourage learning, creativity, and out-of-the-box thinking.

Before earning her PhD from Florida Agricultural and Mechanical University (FAMU) in 2017, Renee became the first mechanical engineering student at the FAMU-Florida State University College of Engineering to be awarded the United States Fulbright Fellowship in 2015. Her journey up to that point was filled with adventure.

Renee was born on the island of Jamaica, in the capital city of Kingston, on January 17, 1984, to Gwendolyn and Glenford. Growing up on the island was fun. She would go on many adventures with her family. Her grandmother, Eulalee, taught Renee all about saving money by using her trusty coin purse. They would sit together on her home's veranda and spread all the different types of coins and paper currency out onto a table. Grandma Eulalee would then pose a variety of situations to Renee, and she would have to figure out the best solution. For example, Renee might be asked to pretend to be buying food for a family of five from the market. Weekend afternoons with her grandmother were not only fun but taught her some valuable skills early on.

Renee attended Holy Rosary Catholic School, where she excelled. She also danced ballet in the afternoon. When she was just 6 years old, her school took a trip to Disney World in Orlando, Florida. When the trip was over, Renee's mother, Gwendolyn, joined her in Florida, and they traveled to New York City, where the rest of the family had already arrived with all their belongings. That was the beginning of her life in the United States.

Growing up in New York City, Renee developed a love for computers, math, and science. She also joined her school's chorus. Renee had to start fresh, yet again, when her family moved to Miami, Florida. She was 11 years old at the time. She entered middle school, where she learned to play the flute. She also joined the Computer Magnet Program, excelling in advanced mathematics courses. In computer class, they learned how to type commands on a computer to make action figures move. Renee had thought she would become a medical surgeon one day. But after taking honors physics in high school and building an electrical circuit

"I NEEDED TO BE AN EXAMPLE FOR THOSE WHO WERE COMING BEHIND ME."

board for a class project, she realized she wanted to become an engineer.

Upon finishing high school with many honors and awards, Renee received several scholarship offers to universities across the country. She chose to attend Florida Agricultural and Mechanical University (FAMU) in Tallahassee, Florida. She planned to major in mechanical engineering and play her flute and piccolo in the FAMU band, known as the Marching 100. Renee chose FAMU because it had a long history of educating African-American students when other universities refused to admit them because of the color of their skin.

Band practice taught her about teamwork, determination, and how to strive for excellence. She was the section leader of the piccolo players. When she saw that one piccolo player was having a hard time correctly memorizing her band music, she sat with the student every day after practice for several weeks to help her memorize the musical repertoire. Little did she know that helping others learn would one day become her life's work.

Renee graduated from college with honors and went on to pursue her PhD in mechanical engineering at the FAMU-Florida State University College of Engineering. Being selected for the United States Fulbright Fellowship Program in 2015 allowed her to study abroad in Nigeria for nine months. There, she taught Nigerian students at the Federal University of Technology at Akure (FUTA) and worked on cutting-edge research projects.

The work Renee conducted while in Nigeria fueled her doctoral dissertation research. She explored the use of a Nigerian plant called cassava to strengthen steel. Cassava is a root vegetable that is very similar to a potato or yam. Renee used the leaves of the cassava in her experiments to increase the strength of steel by placing them together in a furnace. Renee also created a predictive model that can simulate how effective this process would be based on the type of steel used, the furnace temperature, and the amount of time the steel and cassava were in the furnace. This project added value to the world of science because it was renewable, sustainable, and a form of "green" engineering.

Renee graduated with her PhD in mechanical engineering from FAMU in 2017. She had always worked with younger students as a tutor and mentor to help them excel in STEM disciplines. Naturally, she became a mechanical engineering instructor at FAMU, though soon she was named STEM Program Director at Tallahassee Community College (TCC). In that role, she creates and fine-tunes a wide variety of activities for students to gain and keep an interest in pursuing the STEM disciplines in their studies.

Renee recognizes that the world of STEM can be difficult to understand. Yet, the STEM disciplines are essential for solving many problems facing our world today. She tries to ensure that young people are prepared to meet those challenges head-on by fostering understanding of STEM concepts through fun, hands-on activities. At TCC, she exposes students to topics such as computer programming, insect genetics, robotics, virtual reality, artificial intelligence, and battery power. There are many more concepts and innovative techniques worthy of exploration, and Renee is excited about the possibilities that are ahead.

EXPLORE MORE! Read *Girls Think of Everything: Stories of Ingenious Inventions by Women* by Catherine Thimmesh to learn about other women who made innovative discoveries.

TIPS FOR YOU! Renee explored many interests and activities before becoming a scientist. Are you interested in a lot of different things? What do your hobbies teach you about how you want to live your life or what you might like to study later?

POLICE

Gina PRESLEY

{1985– }

Gina Presley is in the prime of her career in forensic science, which is the application of science to the law. Forensic science is used to gather and study deoxyribonucleic acid (DNA), which makes up all living things. DNA is collected from crime scenes and studied to catch criminals or identify victims. It's a fascinating and rewarding career for anyone interested in both science and helping people.

Gina fell in love with science at a very young age. Always fascinated with how things worked, she would often ask for science lab kits and K'nex sets that allowed her to build and be creative at home. Her father was a mechanical engineer, and the two of them loved working on science fair projects together. Her fondest science project memory is winning first place, in fifth grade, for building a dam powered by a real generator. Every summer, her parents enrolled her in a local summer science program, ensuring she had the tools necessary to succeed in college and build a career in science.

Gina's parents and grandparents had all attended Historically Black Colleges and Universities. Gina followed their example and enrolled at Spelman College. Her parents had met there in the seventies, and Gina practically grew up on the campus. She attended nursery school there and later went on to become a member of the Spelman Bronze Dance Troupe. She also was selected for the Howard Hughes Summer Biomedical Program after her junior year of high school and spent six weeks as a student on Spelman's campus. She was elated when she was awarded a full academic scholarship to the college, which was known for helping the most African-American women graduates go on to receive doctorates in science and math. Gina knew Spelman would offer her an environment where she could excel and be surrounded by highly motivated women who looked like her.

While at Spelman College, Gina conducted research in a behavioral neuroscience lab on the effects of dopamine on green tree frogs. Being a city girl, she had to get used to catching her own frogs in local Georgia swamps. She also served as president of the Biology Club and remained active in the surrounding Atlanta community during her college years, giving back to those in need through science-based service projects.

After graduating with a bachelor's degree in biology in 2007, Gina moved to New York City to work as a

National Institutes of Health (NIH) post-baccalaureate research scholar at the Mount Sinai School of Medicine. She worked on research projects in the Department of Community and Preventive Medicine and served as a mentor for local high school students. While Gina loved exploring the Big Apple, she decided—after her first real winter—to head back to a warmer climate.

At the time, a new television series called *CSI: Crime Scene Investigation*, which is a fictional program about forensic scientists, was gaining popularity. In addition, more colleges were starting graduate programs in forensic science. In 2008, Gina became a full-time graduate student in forensic science at the University of Alabama at Birmingham (UAB). There, she examined the effectiveness of different cleaning methods on the recovery of DNA from self-adhesive stamps, which can help solve cases involving suspicious packages, threatening letters, and hate mail. While at UAB, she was chosen for the Graduate Student Spotlight and interned for the Alabama Department of Forensic Sciences. This internship gave her hands-on experience in the world of DNA.

In 2010, Gina received a master's degree in forensic science and was hired full time by the Alabama Department of Forensic Sciences only two weeks after graduation. More than a decade later, Presley continues to work with the Alabama Department of Forensic Sciences as a forensic scientist in the biology section at

> **"HAVING STRONG WOMEN IN MY FAMILY, ESPECIALLY MY DYNAMIC GRANDMOTHER, HELPED MOLD ME. GOING TO COLLEGE AT SPELMAN STRENGTHENED AN ALREADY SOLID FOUNDATION. MY MOTHER, MARY HALL PRESLEY, IS MOST RESPONSIBLE FOR WHO I HAVE BECOME AND THE REASON I CHOSE SPELMAN."**

the Huntsville Regional Laboratory. She was promoted to the position of Huntsville Regional DNA Technical Leader and is the first African-American woman to hold this position at the agency.

As a forensic scientist, Gina examines evidence recovered from crime scenes for the presence of biological stains. These stains go through a DNA analysis process by which a DNA profile is often obtained. DNA is the same no matter where it is found in the body, and, like fingerprints, it is unique to each individual—except in the case of identical twins. This uniqueness allows Gina to compare the DNA found at crime scenes to the DNA of known individuals to search for potential matches. Gina also testifies about her findings in court as an expert witness.

For Gina, helping keep the citizens of Alabama safe by applying her scientific mind and skills to law enforcement is rewarding. In her spare time, she continues to combine her love for science and community service, volunteering at local career fairs and talking about forensic science to both high school and college students. She is a member of the Alabama State Association of Forensic Sciences, the American Academy of Forensic Sciences, the National Spelman Alumnae Association, Alpha Kappa Alpha Sorority, Inc., and The Links, Inc.

EXPLORE MORE! Explore stem-works.com to tour a real forensic biology lab and find other STEM activities.

TIPS FOR YOU! Examine the family room in your home as if it were a crime scene. Plastic sandwich bags, tweezers, and a magnifying glass can help you collect evidence. Use a Sharpie to label the bags with what you collect and where you find it. Pay special attention to items that may hold DNA, such as hair fibers.

Afterword

Now that you've read the book, it's time to have fun! Make slime. Construct a toy train. Make household cleaning products using vinegar, baking soda, and natural oils. Bake from scratch with your friends! Ask your parents about attending a STEM camp. Each time you interact with a cash register, see if you can determine the total amount due with taxes in your head! See if you can figure out how much change you should get back when you use cash. Make up a game with your family to avoid using GPS on trips. Make your own map like Gladys West did! Imagine an app you'd like to invent. Go outside and play!

When it's time, consider attending some of the colleges where the women pioneers in this book studied. Your future is as bright as your brain.

Glossary

agent: a phenomenon, substance, or organism that exerts some force or effect.

aviatrix: a female pilot.

bachelor's degree: awarded by a college, university, or professional school, usually after four years of study.

boycott: to stop buying or using the goods or services of a certain company or country as a protest.

cancer: a disease that occurs when cells that are not normal grow and spread very fast. Normal body cells grow and divide and know to stop growing. Over time, they also die. Unlike normal cells, cancer cells continue to grow and divide out of control and don't die when they're supposed to.

cataracts: a clouding of the normally clear lens of your eye. For people who have cataracts, seeing through cloudy lenses is a bit like looking through a frosty or fogged-up window. Clouded vision caused by cataracts can make it more difficult to read, drive a car (especially at night), or see the expression on a friend's face.

chemotherapy: a treatment with medicines that stop the growth of cancer cells. In most cases, a person gets chemotherapy (chemo) through their veins. The chemo medicine flows into the vein, putting the medicine into the bloodstream, and then the medicine travels throughout the body to attack cancer cells.

civil rights: the basic rights every citizen has under the laws of the government. In the United States, the civil rights of each individual citizen are supposed to be protected by the Constitution regardless of gender, skin color, nationality, age, disability, or religion. Civil rights include the right to free speech, privacy, religion, assembly, a fair trial, and freedom of thought.

discrimination: the unfair treatment of one person or group of people, usually because of the person's gender, religion, nationality, ethnicity (culture), race, or other personal traits. Discrimination prevents people from doing things that other people can do freely.

DNA: the biological material that carries all the information about how a living thing will look and function. DNA in humans determines such things as eye color and lung function. Each piece of information is carried on a different section of the DNA. These sections are called *genes*. DNA is short for deoxyribonucleic acid. It is in every cell of every living thing.

engineer: a person who designs and builds complex products, machines, systems, or structures.

entomology: the scientific study of insects, the largest class of the animal kingdom.

exhibition: a public showing (as of athletic skill or works of art).

follicle: a small tubular cavity containing the root of a hair.

franchise: a contractual relationship between a brand owner (the franchisor) and an independent local business owner (the franchisee).

Great Depression: a period of harsh economic decline in the 1930s, which began in the United States but quickly spread throughout the world. Many people were out of work, hungry, or homeless because of this depression.

hernia: an opening or weakness in the wall of a muscle, tissue, or membrane that normally holds an organ in place.

Historically Black Colleges and Universities (HBCUs): colleges that were established prior to 1964 to educate black Americans barred from study at the majority of the nation's colleges. These institutions continue to provide education for all people and train many who go on to work domestically and internationally as entrepreneurs and in the public and private sectors.

homeopathy: a medical system based on the belief that the body can cure itself. In other words, something that causes symptoms in a healthy person can—in a very small dose—treat an illness with similar symptoms. This is meant to trigger the body's natural defenses.

major: a particular subject of focus at a college or university.

master's degree: an academic degree awarded by a graduate school or department, usually to a person who has completed at least two years of graduate study.

mastery: comprehensive knowledge or skill in a subject.

ocean liner: a passenger ship primarily used as a form of transportation across seas or oceans. Ocean liners may also carry cargo or mail and may sometimes be used for other purposes.

ophthalmologist: a doctor who specializes in diseases and conditions of the eyes, especially things that relate to vision.

ozone layer: the thin part of the Earth's atmosphere that absorbs almost all the Sun's harmful, ultra-violet light.

PhD: a degree awarded to people who have done advanced research into a particular subject. PhD is an abbreviation for doctor of philosophy—the highest degree obtainable in non-medical fields.

race riot: a violent fight between people of different races; a riot caused by racial anger, hatred, etc.

racism: discriminatory or abusive behavior toward members of another race.

radiation: a type of cancer treatment that uses beams of intense energy to kill cancer cells.

research: the careful consideration and study of a particular concern or problem using scientific methods.

rocket science: generally relating to the design and testing of rocket-propelled vehicles, such as orbiting spacecraft or missiles. Rocket scientists specialize in a particular area of aerospace engineering, such as space exploration vehicles or defense systems.

satellite: an artificial body placed in orbit around the Earth or Moon or another planet to collect information or for communication.

solar: relating to or determined by the Sun.

tissue: groups of cells that have similar structures and act together to perform a specific function.

tumor: a growth of abnormal cells that are either malignant or benign.

Quotation Sources

Rebecca Lee Crumpler
Crumpler, Rebecca. *A Book of Medical Discourses.* Boston: Cashman, Keating, printers, 1883.

Annie Turnbo Malone
Malone, Annie T. *Poro in Pictures*. St. Louis: Poro College, 1926.

Bessie Coleman
Chicago Defender, March 10, 1923.

Flemmie Pansy Kittrell
Kittrell, Flemmie. "The Negro Family as a Health Agency," *The Journal of Negro Education* 18, no. 3 (Summer 1949).

Mamie Phipps Clark
Karera, A. 2010. "Profile of Mamie Phipps Clark," in *Psychology's Feminist Voices Multimedia Internet Archive* edited by A. Rutherford. https://www.feministvoices.com/mamie-phipps-clark/.

Katherine Johnson
Johnson, Katherine. "Katherine Johnson, NASA Mathematician." *Makers*. https://www.makers.com/profiles/591f267c6c3f646439558630.

Jane Cooke Wright

Swain, Sandra M. "A Passion for Solving the Puzzle of Cancer: Jane Cooke Wright, MD, 1919–2013." *NCBI*. https://www.ncbi.nlm.nih.gov/pmc/articles/PMC4063385/.

Margaret Strickland Collins

Hunter, Emily. "Field Notes from a Termite Lady." *Smithsonian National Museum of Natural History*. https://nmnh.typepad.com/fieldbooks/2012/11/field-notes-from-a-termite-lady.html.

Gladys West

Butterly, Amelia. "100 Women: Gladys West—the 'Hidden Figure' of GPS." *BBC*. https://www.bbc.com/news/world-43812053.

Annie J. Easley

https://www.nasa.gov/feature/annie-easley-computer-scientist.

Patricia Bath

Associated Press. "Patricia Bath, Pioneering UCLA Ophthalmologist and Inventor, Dies at 76." *Los Angeles Times*, June 5, 2019. https://www.latimes.com/local/obituaries/la-me-ln-cataract-treatment-patricia-bath-20190605-story.html.

Alexa Irene Canady

Canady, Alexa Irene. "Dr. Alexa Irene Canady." *Changing the Face of Medicine*. https://cfmedicine.nlm.nih.gov/physicians/biography_53.html.

Mae Carol Jemison

"Famous Firsts." *Time for Kids*. https://www.timeforkids.com/g34/famous-firsts-3/.

Gina Presley

Interview with author, May 20, 2019.

Renee Gordon

Interview with author, May 17, 2019.

Acknowledgments

Special thanks to: The History Consultants, LLC, and Sonja N. Woods, Archivist at Howard University's Moorland Spingarn Research Center.

About the Author

With a terminal degree in US history from Howard University, **Dr. Kimberly Brown Pellum** specializes in the history of women, black colleges, and the struggle for African-American freedom. Her contributions to publicly accessible history include work at the Smithsonian Institution's National Museum of American History, The Rosa Parks Museum, and Google's Arts & Culture series. She is the director of the digital archives project *Museum of Black Beauty*, and the author of two other children's history books—*Queen Like Me: The True Story of Girls Who Changed the World* and *Superhero Like Me: The True Story of Champions Who Changed the World*. She has taught history as a college professor for more than 10 years.